Gradle Beyond the Basics

Tim Berglund

Beijing · Cambridge · Farnham · Köln · Sebastopol · Tokyo

Gradle Beyond the Basics

by Tim Berglund

Printed in the United States of America.

Published by O'Reilly Media, Inc., 1005 Gravenstein Highway North, Sebastopol, CA 95472.

O'Reilly books may be purchased for educational, business, or sales promotional use. Online editions are also available for most titles (*http://my.safaribooksonline.com*). For more information, contact our corporate/institutional sales department: 800-998-9938 or *corporate@oreilly.com*.

Editors: Mike Loukides and Meghan Blanchette
Production Editor: Kara Ebrahim
Proofreader: Kara Ebrahim

Cover Designer: Randy Comer
Interior Designer: David Futato
Illustrator: Rebecca Demarest

July 2013: First Edition

Revision History for the First Edition:

2013-07-15: First release

See *http://oreilly.com/catalog/errata.csp?isbn=9781449304676* for release details.

ISBN: 978-1-449-30467-6

[LSI]

Table of Contents

Preface

Welcome to *Gradle Beyond the Basics*, the second book in the O'Reilly Gradle series. This book picks up from its predecessor, *Building and Testing with Gradle*, and takes you further into the Gradle programming model. We offer the recipes, techniques, and syntax that make Gradle more than just free-form scripting, and place your build instead on the foundation of a strong domain model. The difference is, it is *your* domain model, not a generic one from some build tool that is ignorant of the specifics of your project.

Having introduced you to the basic elements of Gradle in the first book, we can begin to explore the tool's capabilities a bit more deeply. We will cover four discrete areas of Gradle functionality: file operations, custom Gradle plug-ins, build lifecycle hooks, and dependency management. We assume that you are familiar with the basics of how to use Gradle, and with a keen respect of your time and interest, offer no further introduction to the mechanics of simple Gradle builds. If you are brand new to the topic, you should definitely read *Building and Testing* first.

The Gradle APIs are rich, the possibilities for DSLs matching your domain are abundant, and the path towards finally having a build system that conforms to your product is clear. Let's move forward.

Conventions Used in This Book

The following typographical conventions are used in this book:

Italic
> Indicates new terms, URLs, email addresses, filenames, and file extensions.

`Constant width`
> Used for program listings, as well as within paragraphs to refer to program elements such as variable or function names, databases, data types, environment variables, statements, and keywords.

Constant width bold

Shows commands or other text that should be typed literally by the user.

Constant width italic

Shows text that should be replaced with user-supplied values or by values determined by context.

This icon signifies a tip, suggestion, or general note.

This icon indicates a warning or caution.

Safari® Books Online

Safari Books Online is an on-demand digital library that delivers expert content in both book and video form from the world's leading authors in technology and business.

Technology professionals, software developers, web designers, and business and creative professionals use Safari Books Online as their primary resource for research, problem solving, learning, and certification training.

Safari Books Online offers a range of product mixes and pricing programs for organizations, government agencies, and individuals. Subscribers have access to thousands of books, training videos, and prepublication manuscripts in one fully searchable database from publishers like O'Reilly Media, Prentice Hall Professional, Addison-Wesley Professional, Microsoft Press, Sams, Que, Peachpit Press, Focal Press, Cisco Press, John Wiley & Sons, Syngress, Morgan Kaufmann, IBM Redbooks, Packt, Adobe Press, FT Press, Apress, Manning, New Riders, McGraw-Hill, Jones & Bartlett, Course Technology, and dozens more. For more information about Safari Books Online, please visit us online.

How to Contact Us

Please address comments and questions concerning this book to the publisher:

O'Reilly Media, Inc.
1005 Gravenstein Highway North
Sebastopol, CA 95472
800-998-9938 (in the United States or Canada)

707-829-0515 (international or local)

707-829-0104 (fax)

We have a web page for this book, where we list errata, examples, and any additional information. You can access this page at *http://oreil.ly/gradle-btb*.

To comment or ask technical questions about this book, send email to *bookques tions@oreilly.com*.

For more information about our books, courses, conferences, and news, see our website at *http://www.oreilly.com*.

Find us on Facebook: *http://facebook.com/oreilly*

Follow us on Twitter: *http://twitter.com/oreillymedia*

Watch us on YouTube: *http://www.youtube.com/oreillymedia*

Acknowledgments

I would like to extend my thanks to my team of excellent tech editors who contributed ably to the quality of this book: Jason Porter, Spencer Allain, Darin Pope, and Rod Hilton. Special thanks go to Luke Daley, who didn't just edit, but provided significant rewrites to the chapter on dependency management when the original version didn't quite capture the spirit of the subject matter. Luke was also a willing helper on the other end of a Skype chat window on more than one occasion when I had a technical question about some Gradle internal or other. He is a valued friend with whom I look forward to more collaboration in the future.

Additional thanks go to my friend, Matthew McCullough, for his early contributions to the chapter on Build Hooks. Matthew has a long history in the build tool space, and his insights into build metaprogramming were no small help in getting that chapter right.

Thanks of course to the longsuffering Hans Docktor, who waited perhaps a year longer than expected to get this book. It is likewise always a pleasure to work with him and to call him my friend.

I am obligated to acknowledge my editor, Meghan Blanchette, but in this case the obligation is one I receive willingly. If Meghan and I work together on another book, she may want to create some automation around the emails she sends to me asking if I am going to keep my latest deadline, so frequent are those checkups. I will still enjoy hearing from her.

I tend to write very early in the morning, so my wife, Kari, never actually saw me work on this volume. She did, however, experience more than one spate of her husband falling asleep at 9:00 pm for many days on end so he could wake up early the next day and write. My thanks, and her name in print, is the least I can offer.

To Hannah and Sarah: Proverbs 14:26.

## CHAPTER 1

File Operations

If the most essential operation in a build is to compile code, then surely the second most essential operation is to copy files. A real-world build routinely copies files from place to place, recursing directory trees, pattern-maching filenames, and performing string operations on file content. Gradle exposes a few methods, task types, and interfaces to make file operations flexible and easy. Collectively, these form Gradle's file API.

To explore the file API, we'll start with practical examples of how to use the Copy task. We'll move from there to an exploration of the file-related methods of the Project object, which are available to you anywhere inside a Gradle build. In the process, we'll learn about the FileCollection interface. Finally, we'll look at the ways the file API is used by common Gradle plug-ins—giving us a richer view of otherwise taken-for-granted structures like JAR files and SourceSets.

Copy Task

The Copy task is a task type provided by core Gradle. At execution, a copy task copies files into a destination directory from one or more sources, optionally transforming files as it copies. You tell the copy task where to get files, where to put them, and how to filter them through a configuration block. The simplest copy task configuration looks like Example 1-1.

Example 1-1. A trivial copy task configuration

```
task copyPoems(type: Copy) {
  from 'text-files'
  into 'build/poems'
}
```

The example assumes there is a directory called text-files containing the text of some poems. Running the script with gradle copyPoems puts those files into the build/ poems directory, ready for processing by some subsequent step in the build.

By default, all files in the from directory are included in the copy operation. You can change this by specifying patterns to include or patterns to exclude. Inclusion and exclusion patterns use Ant-style globbing, where ** will recursively match any subdirectory name, and * will match any part of a filename. Include calls are exclusive by default; that is, they assume that all files not named in the include pattern should be excluded. Similarly, exclude calls are inclusive by default—they assume that all files not named in the exclude pattern should be included by default.

When an exclude is applied along with an include, Gradle prioritizes the exclude. It collects all of the files indicated by the include, then removes all of the files indicated by the exclude. As a result, your include and exclude logic should prefer more inclusive include patterns which are then limited by less inclusive exclude patterns.

If you can't express your include or exclude rules in a single pattern, you can call exclude or include multiple times in a single Copy task configuration (Example 1-2). You can also pass a comma-separated list of patterns to a single method call (Example 1-3).

Example 1-2. A copy task that copies all the poems except the one by Henley

```
task copyPoems(type: Copy) {
  from 'text-files'
  into 'build/poems'
  exclude '**/*henley*'
}
```

Example 1-3. A copy task that only copies Shakespeare and Shelley

```
task copyPoems(type: Copy) {
  from 'text-files'
  into 'build/poems'
  include '**/sh*.txt'
}
```

A common build operation is to gather files from several source directories and copy them into one place. To do this, simply include more than one from configuration, as in Example 1-4. Each call to from can even have its own sets of inclusions and exclusions if needed.

Example 1-4. A copy task taking files from more than one source directory

```
task complexCopy(type: Copy) {
  from('src/main/templates') {
    include '**/*.gtpl'
  }
  from('i18n')
```

```
from('config') {
    exclude 'Development*.groovy'
}
into 'build/resources'
}
```

Transforming Directory Structure

The outcome of Example 1-4 is to put all source files into one flat directory, build/
resources. Of course you may not want to flatten all of the source directories; you might
instead want to preserve some of the structure of the source directory trees or even map
the source directories onto a new tree. To do this, we can simply add additional calls to
into inside the from configuration closures. This is shown in Example 1-5.

*Example 1-5. A copy task mapping source directory structure onto a new destination
structure*

```
task complexCopy(type: Copy) {
  from('src/main/templates') {
    include '**/*.gtpl'
    into 'templates'
  }
  from('i18n')
  from('config') {
    exclude 'Development*.groovy'
    into 'config'
  }
  into 'build/resources'
}
```

Note that a top-level call to into is still required—the build file will not run without it
—and the nested calls to into are all relative to the path of that top-level configuration.

If the number of files or the size of the files being copied is large, then a copy task could
be an expensive build operation at execution time. Gradle's incremental build feature
helps reduce the force of this problem. Gradle will automatically incur the full execution
time burden on the first run of the build, but will keep subsequent build times down
when redundant copying is not necessary.

Renaming Files During Copy

If your build has to copy files around, there's a good chance it will have to rename files
in the process. Filenames might need to be tagged to indicate a deployment environment, or might need to be renamed to some standard form from an environment-
specific origin, or might be renamed according to a product configuration specified by
the build. Whatever the reason, Gradle gives you two flexible ways to get the job done:
regular expressions and Groovy closures.

To rename files using regular expressions, we can simply provide a source regex and a destination filename. The source regex will use groups to capture the parts of the filename that should be carried over from the source to the destination. These groups are expressed in the destination filename with the $1/$2 format. For example, to copy some configuration-specific files from a source to a staging directory, see Example 1-6.

Example 1-6. Renaming files using regular expressions

```
task rename(type: Copy) {
  from 'source'
  into 'dest'
  rename(/file-template-(\d+)/, 'production-file-$1.txt')
}
```

To rename files programmatically, we can pass a closure to the rename method (Example 1-7). The closure takes a single parameter, which is the name of the original file. The return value of the closure is the name of the renamed file.

Example 1-7. Renaming files programmatically

```
task rename(type: Copy) {
  from 'source'
  into 'dest'
  rename { fileName ->
    "production-file${(fileName - 'file-template')}"
  }
}
```

 In Groovy, subtracting one string from another string removes the first occurence of the second string from the first. So, 'one two one four' - 'one' will return 'two one four'. This is a quick way to perform a common kind of string processing.

Filtering and Transforming Files

Often the task of a build is not just to copy and rename files, but to perform transformations on the content of the copied files. Gradle has three principal ways of doing this job: the expand() method, the filter() method, and the eachFile() method. We'll consider these in turn.

Keyword Expansion

A common build use case is to copy a set of configuration files into a staging area and to replace some strings in the files as they're copied. A particular configuration file may contain a substantial set of parameters that do not vary by deployment environment, plus a smaller set of parameters that do. As this configuration file is staged from its working directory into the build directory, it would be convenient to replace the deployment-variable strings as a part of the copy. The expand() method is how Gradle does this.

The expand() method takes advantage of the Groovy SimpleTemplateEngine (*http:// bit.ly/11yxrxt*) class. SimpleTemplateEngine adds a keyword substitution syntax to text files similar to the syntax of Groovy string interpolation. Any string inside curly braces preceded by a dollar sign (${string}) is a candidate for substitution. When declaring keyword expansion in a copy task, you must pass a map to the expand() method (Example 1-8). The keys in the map will be matched to the expressions inside curly braces in the copied file, which will be replaced with the map's corresponding values.

Example 1-8. Copying a file with keyword expansion

```
versionId = '1.6'

task copyProductionConfig(type: Copy) {
  from 'source'
  include 'config.properties'
  into 'build/war/WEB-INF/config'
  expand([
    databaseHostname: 'db.company.com',
    version: versionId,
    buildNumber: (int)(Math.random() * 1000),
    date: new Date()
  ])
}
```

 SimpleTemplateEngine has some other features that are exposed to you when you use the expand() method inside a copy task. Consult the online documentation (*http://bit.ly/11yxrxt*) for more details.

Note that the expression passed to the expand() method is a Groovy map literal—it is enclosed by square brackets, and a series of key/value pairs are delimited by commas, with the key and the value themselves separated by colons. In this example, the task doing the expanding is dedicated to preparing a configuration file for the production configuration, so the map can be expressed as a literal. A real-world build may opt for this approach, or may reach out to other, environment-specific config file fragments for the map data. Ultimately, the map passed to expand() can come from anywhere. The fact that the Gradle build file is executable Groovy code gives you nearly unlimited flexibility in deciding on its origin.

It's helpful in this case to take a look at the source file, so we can directly see where the string substitution is happening.

Here's the source file before the copy-with-filter operation:

```
#
# Application configuration file
#
hostname: ${databaseHostname}
appVersion: ${version}
locale: en_us
initialConnections: 10
transferThrottle: 5400
queueTimeout: 30000
buildNumber: ${buildNumber}
buildDate: ${date.format("yyyyMMdd'T'HHmmssZ")}
```

Here's the destination file after the copy-with-filter operation:

```
#
# Application configuration file
#
hostname: db.company.com
appVersion: 1.6
locale: en_us
initialConnections: 10
transferThrottle: 5400
queueTimeout: 30000
buildNumber: 77
buildDate 20120105T162959-0700
```

Filtering Line by Line

The expand() method is perfect for general-purpose string substitution—and even some lightweight elaborations on that pattern—but some file transformations might need to process every line of a file individually as it is copied. This is where the filter() method is useful.

The filter() method has two forms: one that takes a closure, and one that takes a class. We'll look at both, starting with the simpler closure form.

When you pass a closure to filter(), that closure will be called for every line of the filtered file. The closure should perform whatever processing is necessary, then return the filtered value of the line. For example, to convert Markdown text to HTML using MarkdownJ (*http://markdownj.org/*), see Example 1-9.

Example 1-9. Use filter() with a closure to transform a text file as it is copied

```
import com.petebevin.markdown.MarkdownProcessor

buildscript {
  repositories {
    mavenRepo url: 'http://scala-tools.org/repo-releases'
  }
```

```
  dependencies {
    classpath 'org.markdownj:markdownj:0.3.0-1.0.2b4'
  }
}

task markdown(type: Copy) {
  def markdownProcessor = new MarkdownProcessor()
  into 'build/poems'
  from 'source'
  include 'todo.md'
  rename { it - '.md' + '.html'}
  filter { line ->
    markdownProcessor.markdown(line)
  }
}
```

The source file processed by the example code is a short poem with some comments added. It looks like the following:

```
# A poem by William Carlos Williams
so much depends
upon
# He wrote free verse
a red wheel
barrow
# In the imageist tradition
glazed with rain
water
# And liked chickens
beside the white
chickens
```

The copied and filtered file has blank lines instead of comments:

```
so much depends
upon

a red wheel
barrow

glazed with rain
water

beside the white
chickens
```

Gradle gives you great flexibility in per-file filtering logic, but true to its form, it wants to give you tools to keep all of that filter logic out of task definitions. Rather than clutter your build with lots of filter logic, it would be better to migrate that logic into classes of its own, which can eventually migrate out of the build into individual source files with their own automated tests. Let's take the first step in that direction.

Instead of passing a closure to the `filter()` method, we can pass a class instead. The class must be an instance of `java.io.FilterReader`. The Ant API provides a rich set of pre-written `FilterReader` implementations, which Gradle users are encouraged to re-use. The code shown in Example 1-9 could be rewritten as in Example 1-10.

Example 1-10. Use filter() with a custom Ant Filter class to transform a text file as it is copied

```
import org.apache.tools.ant.filters.*
import com.petebevin.markdown.MarkdownProcessor

buildscript {
  repositories {
    mavenRepo url: 'http://scala-tools.org/repo-releases'
  }

  dependencies {
    classpath 'org.markdownj:markdownj:0.3.0-1.0.2b4'
  }
}

class MarkdownFilter extends FilterReader {
  MarkdownFilter(Reader input) {
    super(new StringReader(new MarkdownProcessor().markdown(input.text)))
  }
}

task copyPoem(type: Copy) {
  into 'build/poems'
  from 'source'
  include 'todo.md'
  rename { it - ~/\.md$/ + '.html'}
  filter MarkdownFilter
}
```

Eventually the `MarkdownFilter` class could move out of the build entirely and into a custom plug-in. That is an important topic with a chapter of its own.

Filtering File by File

The `expand()` and `filter()` methods apply the same transformation function to all of the files in the copy scope, but some transformation logic might want to consider each file individually. To handle this case, we have the `eachFile()` method.

The `eachFile()` method accepts a closure, which is executed for every file as it is copied. That closure takes a single parameter, which is an instance of the `FileCopyDetails` (*http://gradle.org/docs/current/javadoc/org/gradle/api/file/FileCopyDetails.html*) interface. `FileCopyDetails` allows you to consider the contents of the copied files one at time. `FileCopyDetails` exposes methods that allow you to rename the file, change its destination path during the copy, exclude it from the copy operation, create duplicate copies at other paths, and interact with the file programmatically as an instance of java.io.File. You can do many of the same things through the Gradle DSL as described previously, but you might prefer in some cases to drop back to direct manipulation. For example, perhaps you have a custom deployment process that copies a directory full of files and accumulates a SHA1 hash of all the file contents, emitting the hash into the destination directory. You might implement that part of the build as in Example 1-11.

Example 1-11. Use eachFile() to accumulate a hash of several files

```
import java.security.MessageDigest;

task copyAndHash(type: Copy) {
  MessageDigest sha1 = MessageDigest.getInstance("SHA-1");

  into 'build/deploy'
  from 'source'
  eachFile { fileCopyDetails ->
    sha1.digest(fileCopyDetails.file.bytes)
  }
  doLast {
    Formatter hexHash = new Formatter()
    sha1.digest().each { b -> hexHash.format('%02x', b) }
    println hexHash
  }
}
```

The File Methods

There are several methods for operating on files that are available in all Gradle builds. These are methods of the Project (*http://bit.ly/18KECoy*) object, which means you can call them from inside any configuration block or task action in a build. There are convenience methods for converting paths into project-relative java.io.File objects, making collections of files, and recursively turning directory trees into file collections. We'll explore each one of them in turn.

file()

The file() (*http://bit.ly/12j8lRT*) method creates a java.io.File (*http://bit.ly/171PNFE*) object, converting the project-relative path to an absolute path. The file() method takes a single argument, which can be a string, a file, a URL, or a closure whose return value is any of those three.

The file() method is useful when a task has a parameter of type File. For example, the Java plug-in provides a task called jar, which builds a JAR file containing the default sourceSet's class files and resources. The task puts the JAR file in a default location under the build directory, but a certain build might want to override that default. The

Jar (*http://bit.ly/1aVNU1W*) task has a property called `destinationDir` for changing this, which one might assume works as in Example 1-12.

Example 1-12. Trying to set the destinationDir property of a Jar task with a string

```
jar {
  destinationDir = 'build/jar'
}
```

However, this build will fail, because `destinationDir` is of type `File`, not `String`. A pedantic solution might look like Example 1-13.

Example 1-13. Trying to set the destinationDir property of a Jar task with a string

```
jar {
  destinationDir = new File('build/jar')
}
```

This build will run, but will not behave predictably in all cases. The `File` constructor will create an absolute path out of the supplied parameter, but the constructor argument will be considered as if it is relative to the directory in which the JVM started up.[1] This directory may change if you are invoking Gradle directly, through the wrapper, through an IDE, or through integration with a Continuous Integration server. The correct solution is to use the `file()` method, as in Example 1-14.

Example 1-14. Setting the destinationDir property of a Jar task using the file() method

```
jar {
  destinationDir = file('build/jar')
}
```

This build results in the `destinationDir` property being set to the `build/jar` directory under the build's project root. This is the expected behavior, and will work regardless of how Gradle is being invoked.

If you already have a `File` object, the `file()` method will attempt to convert it into a project-relative path in the same way. The construction `new File('build/jar')` has no defined parent directory, so `file(new File('build/jar'))` will force its parent to the build's project root directory. This example shows an awkward construction—real code would likely omit the inner `File` construction—but `file()`'s operation on `File` objects works as the example shows. You might use this case if you already had the `File` object lying around for some reason.

`file()` can also operate on `java.net.URL` (*http://bit.ly/12fh2ci*) and `java.net.URI` (*http://bit.ly/12oyAl8*) objects whose `protocol` or `scheme` is `file://`. File URLs are not

---

1. This is an implementation detail not specified by the documentation for `java.io.File`. It is common behavior, but even this much cannot be assumed between environments.

a common case, but they often show up when resources are being loaded through the ClassLoader (*http://bit.ly/12j8ULi*). If you happen to encounter a file URL in your build, you can easily convert it to a project-relative File object with the file() method.

files()

The files() (*http://bit.ly/16n2gS6*) method returns a collection of files based on the supplied parameters. It is like file() in that it attempts to produce project-relative absolute paths in the File objects it creates, but it differs in that it operates on collections of files. It takes a variety of different parameter types as inputs, as shown in Table 1-1.

Table 1-1. The parameters accepted by files()

Parameter type	Method behavior
String	Creates a collection containing a single, project-relative file. Resolves filenames just like file().
java.io.File (*http://docs.oracle.com/javase/6/docs/api/java/io/File.html*)	Creates a collection containing a single, project-relative file. Resolves File objects just like file().
java.net.URL (*http://docs.oracle.com/javase/6/docs/api/java/net/URL.html*) or java.net.URI (*http://docs.oracle.com/javase/6/docs/api/java/net/URI.html*)	Creates a collection of the indicated file. Supports only file:// URLs, just like file().
Collection, Iterable, or Array	Creates a file collection containing all of the named files. Collection elements are recursively resolved, so they may contain any of the other datatypes allowed by files(). EXAMPLES: `// A Groovy ArrayList literal` `files(['src/main/groovy','src/test/groovy'])` `// listFiles() returns an array of File objects` `files(file('src/changelog/resources').listFiles())`
Task	Produces a file collection of the task's outputs. Output file sets are defined on a per-task basis. Tasks provided by core plug-ins typically have implicit output file sets. EXAMPLE (using the Java plug-in): `// Evaluates to the Java compiler's output directory` `files(compileJava)`
Task Outputs	Behaves the same as a task name, but allows the TaskOutputs object to be named explicitly. EXAMPLE (using the Java plug-in): `// Evaluates to the Java compiler's output directory` `files(compileJava.outputs)`

As you can see, `files()` is an incredibly versatile method for creating a collection of files. It can take filenames, file objects, file URLs, Gradle tasks, or Java collections containing any of the same.

Beginning Gradle developers often expect the return type of the method to be a trivial collection class that implements `List`. It turns out that `files()` returns a `FileCollection`, which is a foundational interface for file programming in Gradle. We will turn our attention to the section on file collections.

fileTree()

The `file()` method is an effective way to turn paths into files, and the `files()` method builds on this to build lists of of files that can be managed as collections. But what about when you want to traverse a directory tree and collect all the files you find, and work with those as a collection? This is a job for the `fileTree()` method.

There are three ways to invoke `fileTree()`, and each of them borrows heavily from the configuration of the copy task. They all have several features in common: the method must be pointed to a root directory to traverse, and may optionally be given patterns to include or exclude.

The simplest use of `fileTree()` simply points it at a parent directory, allowing it to recurse through all subdirectories and add all of the files it finds into the resulting file collection. For example, if you wanted to create a collection of all of the production source files in a Java project, the expression `fileTree('src/main/java')` would get the job done.

Alternatively, you might want to perform some simple filtering to include some files and exclude others. Suppose, for example, that you knew that some backup files with the ~ extension were likely to exist in the source files. Furthermore, you knew some XML files were mixed in with the source files (rather than placed in the `resources` source set where they belong), and you wanted to focus on that XML. You could create file collections to deal with both of the cases shown in Example 1-15.

Example 1-15. Using fileTree() with includes and excludes

```
def noBackups = fileTree('src/main/java') {
  exclude '**/*~'
}

def xmlFilesOnly = fileTree('src/main/java') {
  include '**/*.xml'
}
```

Alternatively, the directory and the include and exclude patterns can be provided in map form, as shown in Example 1-16. The use of this syntax in place of the closure configuration syntax is a matter of style.

Example 1-16. Using fileTree() with includes and excludes given in a map literal

```
def noBackups = fileTree(dir: 'src/main/java', excludes: ['**/*~'])
def xmlFilesOnly = fileTree(dir: 'src/main/java', includes: ['**/*.xml'])
```

The FileCollection Interface

If you tried running the examples in the the section on the files method and you poked around at them just a little bit, you may have noticed that the return value of the `files()` and `fileTree()` methods don't have a very friendly default `toString()` implementation (Example 1-17). If they were simply ArrayLists as intuition would suggest, we would expect a dump of their contents. The fact that we don't see this is a hint to something useful going on in the Gradle API (Example 1-18).

Example 1-17. The default toString() implementation of a FileCollection

```
task copyPoems(type: Copy) {
  from 'text-files'
  into 'build/poems'
}

println "NOT HELPFUL:"
println files(copyPoems)
```

Here's the output of the previous build, showing default `toString()` behavior:

```
$ gradle -b file-collection-not-helpful.gradle
NOT HELPFUL:
file collection
```

Example 1-18. A more useful way to look at a FileCollection

```
task copyPoems(type: Copy) {
  from 'text-files'
  into 'build/poems'
}

println "HELPFUL:"
println files(copyPoems).files
```

Here's the output of the previous build, showing the contents of the `FileCollection`:

```
$ gradle -b file-collection-helpful.gradle
HELPFUL:
[~/oreilly-gradle-book-examples/file-operations-lab/build/poems]
```

The object returned by the files() method is not a List, but a FileCollection.[2] The FileCollection type shows up in many other places in Gradle: in the contents of SourceSet objects, in task inputs and outputs, in Java classpaths, in dependency configurations, and more. Knowing the essential methods of the type goes a long way in equipping you to program file operations effectively, whether the files are transitive JAR dependencies fetched from a Maven repository, source files in the build of a Groovy project, or static resources in a web application. We will explore the key operations supported by the interface here.

To illustrate these features, we'll start with a common build file that sets up some interesting collections of files (Example 1-19). We'll add a task at a time to this example build to see each feature.

Example 1-19. The base build from which we will derive FileCollection examples

```
apply plugin: 'java'

repositories {
  mavenCentral()
}

dependencies {
  compile 'org.springframework:spring-context:3.1.1.RELEASE'
}
```

Converting to a Set

We've already seen the files property of FileCollection. It returns an object of type Set<File> containing all of the files or directories in the file collection. To list all of the source files in the previous project, we might add the task seen in Example 1-20.

Example 1-20. A naive way to list source files

```
task naiveFileLister {
  doLast {
    println fileTree('src/main/java').files
  }
}
```

Here's the result of the naiveFileLister task:

```
$ gradle nFL
:naiveFileLister
[~/file-collection-lab/src/main/java/org/gradle/example/ConsoleContentSink.java,
~/file-collection-lab/src/main/java/org/gradle/example/Content.java,
```

---

2. There are actually several subtypes of FileCollection that may be in use in any of these cases. The behavior of these supertypes may be important in some cases, but we'll confine our attention to the common supertype here.

```
~/file-collection-lab/src/main/java/org/gradle/example/ContentFactory.java,
~/file-collection-lab/src/main/java/org/gradle/example/ContentRegistry.java,
~/file-collection-lab/src/main/java/org/gradle/example/ContentSink.java,
~/file-collection-lab/src/main/java/org/gradle/example/
   DefaultContentFactory.java,
~/file-collection-lab/src/main/java/org/gradle/example/DonneContent.java,
~/file-collection-lab/src/main/java/org/gradle/example/PoetryEmitter.java,
~/file-collection-lab/src/main/java/org/gradle/example/ShakespeareContent.java]

BUILD SUCCESSFUL
```

Converting to a Path String

A build can manipulate collections of files for various purposes, which sometimes include using the collection with an operating system command that expects a list of files. Internally, the core Java plug-in does this with compile-time dependencies when executing the `javac` compiler (Example 1-21). The Java compiler has a command-line switch for specifying the classpath, and that switch must be provided with an operating-specific string. The `asPath` property converts a `FileCollection` into this OS-specific string.

Example 1-21. Printing out all of the compile-time dependencies of the build as a path-like string

```
println configurations.compile.asPath
```

Here's the results of the build with the previous addition:

```
$ gradle

~/.gradle/caches/artifacts-8/filestore/org.springframework/spring-context/
3.1.1.RELEASE/jar/ecb0784a0712c1bfbc1c2018eeef6776861300e4/spring-
context-3.1.1.RELEASE.jar:
~/.gradle/caches/artifacts-8/filestore/org.springframework/spring-asm/
3.1.1.RELEASE/jar/8717ad8947fcada5c55da89eb474bf053c30e57/spring-
asm-3.1.1.RELEASE.jar:
~/.gradle/caches/artifacts-8/filestore/commons-logging/commons-logging/
1.1.1/jar/5043bfebc3db072ed80fbd362e7caf00e885d8ae/commons-logging-1.1.1.jar:
~/.gradle/caches/artifacts-8/filestore/org.springframework/spring-core/
3.1.1.RELEASE/jar/419e9233c8d55f64a0c524bb94c3ba87e51e7d95/spring-
core-3.1.1.RELEASE.jar:
~/.gradle/caches/artifacts-8/filestore/org.springframework/spring-beans/
3.1.1.RELEASE/jar/83d0e5adc98714783f0fb7d8a5e97ef4cf08da49/spring-
beans-3.1.1.RELEASE.jar:
~/.gradle/caches/artifacts-8/filestore/aopalliance/aopalliance/1.0/jar/
235ba8b489512805ac13a8f9ea77a1ca5ebe3e8/aopalliance-1.0.jar:
~/.gradle/caches/artifacts-8/filestore/org.springframework/spring-aop/
3.1.1.RELEASE/jar/3c86058cdaea30df35e4b951a615e09eb07da589/spring-
aop-3.1.1.RELEASE.jar:
~/.gradle/caches/artifacts-8/filestore/org.springframework/spring-expression/
```

```
3.1.1.RELEASE/jar/1486d7787ec4ff8da8cbf8752d30e4c808412b3f/spring-
expression-3.1.1.RELEASE.jar
```

Module Dependencies as FileCollections

The most convenient way to illustrate converting a `FileCollection` to a path-like string is to use a collection of module dependencies, as shown in converting to a path string. It's worth pointing out explicitly that dependency configurations are themselves `File Collections`. When dependencies are listed in the `dependencies { }` section of the build, they are always assigned to a named configuration. Configurations are themselves defined in the `configurations { }` section of the build.[3]

As a teacher and frequent conference presenter on Gradle, sometimes I want to enable students to build Java code at times when there is no reliable internet connection. (Many US hotels and conference centers are still woefully unprepared for a few hundred software developers, each with two or three devices on the wireless network and a seemingly insatiable appetite for bandwidth.) While I strongly prefer dependencies to be managed by my build tool, it might make sense for me to prepare lab materials with all of the dependencies statically located in the project in the style of old Ant builds.[4] For some Java frameworks and APIs, chasing all of these JARs down by hand can be a burden. By using module dependencies as file collections, we can automate this work.

If we add the following trivial copy task to Example 1-19, we'll find the `lib` directory quickly populated with all of the JARs we need after we run the task. Adding new dependencies to the project later will require only that we re-run the task, and the new JARs will appear as expected. Note that the `from` method of the `Copy` task configuration block, which took a directory name as a string in previous examples, can also take a `FileCollection` as shown in Example 1-22.

Example 1-22. Using module dependencies as a FileCollection to capture JAR files.

```
task copyDependencies(type: Copy) {
  from configurations.compile
  into 'lib'
}
```

---

3. The most commonly used dependency configurations are `compile` and `runtime`, which are defined by the Java plug-in, and not explicitly inside a `configurations` block. For a full treatment of configurations and dependencies, see Chapter 4.

4. You may prefer this scheme over repositories like Maven Central on principal. Gradle does not force you to use one mechanism of the other.

Adding and Subtracting FileCollections

FileCollections can also be added and subtracted using the + and - operators. We can derive a set of examples by using dependency configurations as file collections.

Our example build for this section is a command-line application using the Spring framework. Spring brings with it a half dozen or so JARs in the minimal case, which would be fairly painful to provide on the command line every time we wanted to run the application. The JavaExec (*http://bit.ly/184LhHv*) task provides us with a convenient way to solve the problem, as long as we can tell it the class to run and the classpath it should use when launching the new Java Virtual Machine (Example 1-23).

The classpath we want has two components: all of the compile-time dependencies of the project[5] plus the classes compiled from the main Java sources of the project. The former are available in the configurations.compile collection, and the latter in sourceSets.main.output. We will explore sourceSet collections more in the next section.

Example 1-23. Using FileCollection addition to create a runtime classpath

```
task run(type: JavaExec) {
  main = 'org.gradle.example.PoetryEmitter'
  classpath = configurations.compile + sourceSets.main.output
}
```

Subtracting one file collection from another creates a new collection containing all of the files in the left-hand collection that are not also in the right-hand collection. To create a collection of all of the text resources in our example build that are not Shelley poetry, we might add the code in Example 1-24 to our build.

Example 1-24. Creating an intersection of two FileCollections

```
def poems = fileTree(dir: 'src/main/resources', include: '*.txt')
def romantics = fileTree(dir: 'src/main/resources', include: 'shelley*')
def goodPoems = poems - romantics
```

Printing out the files property of goodPoems (or otherwise inspecting the contents of the collection) shows that it contains all of the .txt files in the src/main/resources directory, but not the file whose name starts with shelley. In a practical build, this case might be accomplished with an excludes property, but more subtle intersections of FileCollections are also possible, such as subtracting container-provided JARs from the set of dependencies packaged up by a WAR task when building a Java web application.

---

5. Compile-time dependencies are, by definition, run-time dependencies as well.

SourceSets as FileCollections

In earlier examples, we used the `fileTree()` method to create a file collection of all of the source files in a project. It turns out that Gradle gives us a much cleaner way to get this same job done, using the same interface as we've been using all along. Source Sets (*http://gradle.org/docs/current/dsl/org.gradle.api.tasks.SourceSet.html*) are the domain objects Gradle uses to represent collections of source files, and they happen to expose source code inputs and compiled outputs as `FileCollections`.

The `allSource` property of a `SourceSet` object returns a file collection containing all source inputs and, in the case of source sets compiled by the Java plug-in, all resource files as well. In our example build, inspecting the property would yield the results in Example 1-25.

Example 1-25. Printing out the collection of source files in the main Java SourceSet

```
println sourceSets.main.allSource.files

    [~/file-collection-lab/src/main/resources/application-context.xml,
    ~/file-collection-lab/src/main/resources/chesterton.txt,
    ~/file-collection-lab/src/main/resources/henley.txt,
    ~/file-collection-lab/src/main/resources/shakespeare.txt,
    ~/file-collection-lab/src/main/resources/shelley.txt,
    ~/file-collection-lab/src/main/java/org/gradle/example/ConsoleContentSink.java,
    ~/file-collection-lab/src/main/java/org/gradle/example/Content.java,
    ~/file-collection-lab/src/main/java/org/gradle/example/ContentFactory.java,
    ~/file-collection-lab/src/main/java/org/gradle/example/ContentRegistry.java,
    ~/file-collection-lab/src/main/java/org/gradle/example/ContentSink.java,
    ~/file-collection-lab/src/main/java/org/gradle/example/
      DefaultContentFactory.java,
    ~/file-collection-lab/src/main/java/org/gradle/example/DonneContent.java,
    ~/file-collection-lab/src/main/java/org/gradle/example/PoetryEmitter.java,
    ~/file-collection-lab/src/main/java/org/gradle/example/ShakespeareContent.java]
```

Likewise, the build outputs are provided in the `outputs` property. The outputs are not given as an exhaustive list of all of the files generated by the compiler—this would require that we run the compiler before interpreting the source set—but instead as a list of the directories into which compiled outputs will be placed (Example 1-26).

Example 1-26. Printing out the output directories the Java compiler will use for the main source set.

```
println sourceSets.main.output.files

    [~/file-collection-lab/build/classes/main,
    ~/file-collection-lab/build/resources/main]
```

Lazy Files

When programming with file collections, it might be tempting to think of them as static lists. For example, a call to `fileTree()` might scan the filesystem at the time it is called, producing an immutable list that the build can then manipulate. Immutable data structures have their uses, but in the Gradle lifecycle, this would make file collections difficult to use. As a result, instances of the `FileCollection` interface are lazily evaluated whenever it is meaningful to do so.

For example, a task could use the `fileTree()` method to create a collection of all of the files in the `build/main/classes` directory that match the glob pattern `**/*Test.class`. If that file collection is created during the configuration phase (which is likely),[6] the files it is attempting to find may not exist until deep into the execution phase. Hence, file collections are designed to be static descriptions of the collection semantics, and the actual contents of the collection are not materialized until they are needed at a particular time in the build execution.

Conclusion

In this chapter, we've looked at Gradle's comprehensive support for file operations. We explored copy tasks, seeing their ability to move files around in trivial and non-trivial ways, performing various kinds of pattern-matching on files, and even filtering file contents during copy. We looked at keyword expansion and line-by-line filtering of file contents during copy, and also at renaming files as they're copied—something that often comes in handy when modifying the contents of copied files. We reviewed the three important methods Gradle developers use to deal with files, and finally learned about the all-important `FileCollection` interface that describes so many important Gradle domain objects. Gradle doesn't leave you with the bare semantics of the Java `File` object, but gives you a rich set of APIs to do the kinds of file programming you're likely to do as you create custom builds and automation pipelines in your next-generation builds.

---

6. Gradle builds have three phases: initialization, configuration, and execution. Configuration-time build code sets up the task graph for Gradle to process. Actual build activity like copying, compiling, and archiving takes place during the execution phase.

## CHAPTER 2

Custom Plug-Ins

Plug-In Philosophy

With its standard domain-specific language (DSL) and core plug-ins, Gradle intends to be a powerful build tool without the addition of any extensions or add-ons. Most common build tasks can be accomplished with these tools as configured by simple build files. Common builds are easy to write; however, common builds are not so common.[1]

Projects that begin as simple collections of source files and a few static resources bundled into a standard archive format often evolve into complex multi-project hierarchies with requirements to perform database migration, execute repetitive transformations of static resources, perform and validate automated deployments, and accomplish still more build automation that doesn't always easily conform to an existing standard or set of parameters.

Developing such a build is a specialized form of software development. The software in question is not the code that automates the business domain of the project itself, but code that automates the *build* domain of the project. This specialized code is software nevertheless, and it is precisely this kind of development that Gradle aims to facilitate.

To write this kind of code, an untutored Gradle developer might simply write a large amount of imperative Groovy code inside `doLast()` clauses of a build file. However, this code would be untestable, and would lead to large and unreadable build files of the kind other build tools are often criticized for creating. This practice is strongly discouraged. In its place, we offer the plug-in API.

---

1. With apologies to Kurt Vonnegut.

The Plug-In API

A Gradle plug-in is a distributable archive that extends the core functionality of Gradle. Plug-ins extend Gradle in three ways. First, a plug-in can program the underlying `Project` (*http://bit.ly/150gDg3*) object just as if an additional build file were mixed into the current build file. Tasks, `SourceSets`, dependencies, repositories, and more can be added or modified by applying a plug-in.

Second, a plug-in can bring new modules into the build to perform specialized work. A plug-in that creates WSDL files from an annotated Java web service implementation should not include its own code for scanning for annotations and generating content in a specialized XML vocabulary, but should instead declare a dependency on an existing library to do that work, and provide a mechanism for that library to be fetched from an online repository if it is not already present on the build system.

Finally, plug-ins can introduce new keywords and domain objects into the Gradle build language itself. There is nothing in the standard DSL to describe the servers to which a deployment might be targeted, the database schemas associated with the application, or the operations exposed by an underlying source control tool. Indeed, the standard DSL can't possibly envision every scenario and domain that build developers may encounter. Instead, Gradle opts to provide a well-documented API that allows you, the build developer, to extend Gradle's standard build language in ways that are entirely customized to your context. This is a core strength of Gradle as a build tool. It allows you to write concise, declarative builds in an idiomatic language backed by rich, domain-specific functionality. This is accomplished through plug-ins.

The Example Plug-In

In this chapter, we will create a Gradle plug-in to automate the use of the open-source database refactoring tool, Liquibase (*http://liquibase.org/*). Liquibase is a command-line tool written in Java whose purpose is to manage change in a relational database schema. It can reverse-engineer an existing database schema into its XML change log, and track the version of that change log against running instances of the database scheme to determine whether any new database refactorings must be applied. For users who prefer a Groovy syntax over XML, an open-source Groovy Liquibase DSL (*https://github.com/tlberglund/groovy-liquibase*) is available.

You can learn more about Liquibase online at the Liquibase Quick Start (*http://liqui base.org/quickstart*).

Liquibase is very good at what it does, but it is cumbersome to execute from the command line without a wrapper script of some kind. Moreover, since a high level of build and deployment automation is always an implicit goal, we would prefer to be able to wire Liquibase operations into our build lifecycle.

Our goals in this chapter will be to do the following:

- Create Gradle tasks corresponding to the `generateChangeLog`, `changeLogSync`, and `update` commands (*http://bit.ly/13UpTVW*) inside a Gradle build file.
- Make the Groovy DSL available to replace the default XML Changelog format.
- Refactor the Gradle tasks into a custom task type.
- Introduce Gradle DSL extensions to describe Changelogs and database configurations.
- Package the plug-in as a distributable JAR file.

The Liquibase plug-in will begin its life as a standard Gradle build file. This is an easy way to begin sketching out and prototyping code whose final form you do not yet know, which is a typical workflow in the development of new forms of build automation. As the plug-in takes shape, we will slowly refactor it into a distributable plug-in project with a lifecycle of its own. Evolving plug-in development in this manner is a perfectly appropriate, low-ceremony path to learning the API and discovering the requirements of your build extension.

Setup

To run the example code in this chapter, you'll need a database for Liquibase to connect to. The book's example code has a build file that sets up the H2 database (*http://bit.ly/1buVHCE*) for this purpose. Using Git, clone the *http://github.com/gradleware/oreilly-gradle-book-examples* repository, then change to the `plugins/database-setup` directory. Run the following two tasks:

```
$ gradle -b database.gradle createDatabaseScript
$ gradle -b database.gradle buildSchema
```

The first command will provide a platform-specific script called `starth2` that will run the H2 embedded database administrative console for you to inspect the schema at any time during plug-in development. The second command will create a sample database schema in desperate need of refactoring—just the kind of test environment we'll need for our plug-in development.

 You will have to move the `database.gradle` build file to the directory in which you are doing plug-in development, and execute the `build Schema` task from there to ensure that the H2 database is in the right location for your plug-in to find it. Alternatively, you can place the database in a directory outside of your development directory and edit the JDBC URL to point to the correct path, but this step is left as an exercise for the reader.

Sketching Out Your Plug-In

Our Liquibase plug-in begins with the need to create tasks to perform Changelog reverse engineering, Changelog synchronization, and updating of the Changelog against the database. Some digging into the Liquibase API shows that the best way to run these three commands is to call the `liquibase.integration.commandline.Main.main()` method. This method expects an array of command-line arguments indicating the database to connect to and which Liquibase sub-command to run. For each of its tasks that perform some Liquibase action, our plug-in will end up constructing this array and calling this method.

It's worth thinking about precisely what those tasks might be. Given that we plan to support three Liquibase commands—`generateChangeLog`, `changeLogSync`, and `update`—we can plan on creating three tasks by those same names. In a different scenario, you might decide to "namespace" the task names by prefixing them with `lb` or `liquibase` to keep them from colliding with tasks from other plug-ins, but for our purposes here we can keep the task names short and simple.

We also know we're going to introduce some custom DSL syntax to describe databases and ChangeLogs, but let's keep that as a footnote for now. We'll revisit the idea and decide what that syntax should look like as soon as we're ready to implement it.

Custom Liquibase Tasks

Our plug-in will eventually introduce some fully-implemented tasks that call Liquibase with little or no declarative configuration. Before it can do that, though, we will need to build a custom task type. The purpose of this task is to convert task parameters into the required argument list for the Liquibase command line entry point and call the `main()` method. The implementation is shown in Example 2-1.

Example 2-1. The Liquibase task type prototype

```
import org.gradle.api.DefaultTask
import org.gradle.api.tasks.TaskAction
import liquibase.integration.commandline.Main

class LiquibaseTask extends DefaultTask {
  String command
  String url, password, username
  File changeLog

  @TaskAction
  def liquibaseAction() {
    def args = [
      "--url=${url}",
      "--password=${password}",
      "--username=${username}",
      "--changeLogFile=${changeLog.absolutePath}",
```

```
      command
    ]

    Main.main(args as String[])
  }
}
```

Remember, a custom task type is simply a class that implements the `org.gradle.api.Task` interface, or more commonly extends the `org.gradle.api.De faultTask` base class. The `LiquibaseTask` provides a basic interface between the rest of the build and the core action of executing the Liquibase command-line driver through which all Liquibase operations are normally accessed. The properties of the `Liquibase Task` will become task configuration parameters when the plug-in tasks are used in an actual build later on.

Having defined the custom task, we need only to create an actual task having that type, and to configure it. Note in Example 2-2 that we can use Gradle's configuration syntax to set instance variables in the task class. We assign values to the `url`, `username`, `pass word`, `changeLog`, and `command` properties through a very standard assignment syntax.

Example 2-2. Instantiating the custom Liquibase task

```
task generateChangeLog(type: LiquibaseTask) {
  url = 'jdbc:h2:db/gradle_plugins'
  username = 'secret'
  password = 'sa'
  changeLog = file('changelog.xml')
  command = 'generateChangeLog'
}
```

Applying Yourself

Now that we've got a custom task type that makes it possible to run Liquibase from Gradle, let's take a step back and begin building the plug-in proper. The simplest Gradle plug-in is a class that implements the `org.gradle.api.Plugin<Project>` interface. That interface defines a single method: `void apply(Project project)`. We could begin with a method like what we see in Example 2-3.

 The `Plugin` interface is type-parameterized because plug-ins can theoretically be applied to any kind of Gradle object. Applying them to `Project` is by far the most common use case, and is the only one we'll look at here.

Example 2-3. The apply() method of the first version of the Liquibase plug-in

```
class LiquibasePlugin implements Plugin<Project> {
  void apply(Project project) {
    project.task('generateChangeLog', type: LiquibaseTask) {
      group = 'Liquibase'
      command = 'generateChangeLog'
    }
    project.task('changeLogSync', type: LiquibaseTask) {
      group = 'Liquibase'
      command = 'changeLogSync'
    }
    project.task('update', type: LiquibaseTask) {
      group = 'Liquibase'
      command = 'update'
    }
  }
}
```

As a reminder, when you are first sketching out a plug-in as we are doing, you can code this class and the associated `LiquibaseTask` class directly in your `build.gradle` file. At this point in development, you are trying to learn the plug-in API and the scope and design of your plug-in itself. Deployment and packaging will eventually be very important concerns, but we can happily ignore them for now.

This example creates three new build tasks: `generateChangeLog`, `changeLogSync`, and `update`.[2] Since the Liquibase plug-in is written in Groovy, we're able to use a very Gradle-like syntax to declare new tasks; indeed, the code shown here would work *verbatim* inside a build file, apart from any plug-in definition. Build masters don't have to write plug-ins in Groovy, but it's a rewarding choice due to its similarity to the Gradle build file syntax and its productivity advantages over Java as a language.

Extensions

At this point our plug-in is starting to be able to do some work, but its configuration is rather pedantic (Example 2-4). We must configure each and every task with the database username, password, URL, and the changelog file.

Example 2-4. The Liquibase-enabled build so far

```
generateChangeLog {
  url = 'jdbc:h2:db/gradle_plugin'
  password = 'secret'
  username = 'sa'
  changeLog = file('changelog.xml')
}
```

---

2. In Liquibase, `generateChangeLog` reverse engineers a database schema, `changeLogSync` places a new database under Liquibase's control, and `update` pushes new changes into a database.

```
changeLogSync {
  url = 'jdbc:h2:db/gradle_plugin'
  password = 'secret'
  username = 'sa'
  changeLog = file('changelog.xml')
}

update {
  url = 'jdbc:h2:db/gradle_plugin'
  password = 'secret'
  username = 'sa'
  changeLog = file('changelog.xml')
}
```

Clearly, we shouldn't settle for this. The real power of Gradle plug-ins comes not just from the ability to hide a bunch of imperative code behind a plug-in declaration—custom Ant tasks and Maven plug-ins had already accomplished this a decade before Gradle had its 1.0 release—but rather from the ability to extend the domain model of the build. The Extension API is the primary means of doing so.

Design of plug-in extensions should begin with a sketch of what the desired build file syntax will look like. To design our build file syntax, we must first imagine what sorts of things our build will interact with in its now-expanding domain. In this case, this is simple: the build needs to know about databases and changelogs.

A database is a particular instance of a JDBC-connected database. A build automated with Liquibase database migrations will have separate domain objects representing the local database sandbox, a database instance on a staging server used for ad-hoc testing, a production database instance, and so on.

A Liquibase changelog is a file containing an ordered list of all of the refactorings performed on the database, expressed in an XML format. You can read more about Liquibase changelogs (*http://www.liquibase.org/documentation/databasechangelog*) on the Liquibase site. Example 2-5 will have a single changelog, but real-world builds using Liquibase may break up their database refactorings into two, three, four, or more separate files. Our domain model must support any number of changelog files.

Example 2-5. The goal of our plug-in's new DSL.

```
liquibase {
  changelogs {
    main {
      file = file('changelog.groovy')
    }
  }

  databases {
    sandbox {
      url = 'jdbc:h2:db/liquibase_workshop;FILE_LOCK=NO'
```

```
      username = 'sa'
      password = ''
    }
    staging {
      url = 'jdbc:mysql://staging.server/app_db'
      username = 'dev_account'
      password = 'ab87d24bdc7452e557'
    }
  }

  defaultDatabase = databases.sandbox
}
```

Note what we have done here: we have proposed new Gradle build syntax for describing new domain objects not originally envisioned by the designers of Gradle. All of this new syntax is contained within a fixed namespace (liquibase), but otherwise we have significant control over what it looks like and how it represents our domain. This deceptively simple observation is at the heart of the value of Gradle as a platform for creating customized builds. Gradle allows us not just to add custom code to our builds, but to add *custom language* as well. This is a key enabling feature for managing build complexity.

Plug-in extensions can hide complexity from build users by exposing a simple, idiomatic DSL in the build—and it isn't even difficult to implement them. An extension takes the form of a class, usually written in Java or Groovy, that exposes the properties and methods accessed in the extension block. Our example, written in Groovy, is shown in Example 2-6.

Example 2-6. The Liquibase plug-in extension class

```
import org.gradle.api.NamedDomainObjectContainer

class LiquibaseExtension {
  final NamedDomainObjectContainer<Database> databases
  final NamedDomainObjectContainer<ChangeLog> changelogs
  Database defaultDatabase
  String context

  LiquibaseExtension(databases, changelogs) {
    this.databases = databases
    this.changelogs = changelogs
  }

  def databases(Closure closure) {
    databases.configure(closure)
  }

  def changelogs(Closure closure) {
    changelogs.configure(closure)
```

```
    }
}
```

The extension class defines two methods and two non-final properties.[3] The two Name
dDomainObjectContainer instances, databases and changelogs, will hold collections
of domain objects created in the build syntax shown in Example 2-5. NamedDomainOb
jectContainer is a generic collection, and each instance holds domain objects of a
different type. The Database and ChangeLog classes will have to be defined as shown in
Example 2-7. The only feature that sets them apart from regular POJOs[4] (or POGOs)
is that they must have a property called name and a constructor that accepts a String
and initializes the name property with it. Otherwise they do not extend any base class
or implement any interface in the Gradle API.

The Liquibase-enabled Gradle build is able to maintain collections of databases and
changelogs because of these two classes, and the way they are included in the extension
class through the NamedDomainObjectContainer collection.

Example 2-7. The Database and ChangeLog classes

```
class ChangeLog
{
  def name
  def file
  def description

  ChangeLog(String name) {
    this.name = name
  }
}

class Database
{
  def name
  def url
  def username
  def password

  Database(String name) {
    this.name = name
  }
}
```

---

3. In Java and Groovy, final fields can be initialized when the object is constructed, but can't be changed
   thereafter. These two final fields are object collections, and the objects in the collections can be changed at
   runtime, but the collection instances themselves are fixed once the object is constructed.

4. POJO stands for Plain Old Java Object. It refers to a Java object whose type consists only of properties,
   methods, and an ordinary constructor, with no external requirement on a runtime container to create instances of it.

To apply this extension to the projects that use our plug-in, we will have to modify our LiquibasePlugin.apply() method. The enhanced apply() method can be seen in Example 2-8. The new functionality is in at the end, where the extensions.create() method is called. This method call indicates that the extension context will be named liquibase, and passes in the instances of the NamedDomainObjectContainers that will be held by the extension object.

Example 2-8. The apply() method with the plug-in extension included

```
class LiquibasePlugin implements Plugin<Project> {
  void apply(Project project) {
    // Create and install custom tasks
    project.task('generateChangeLog', type: LiquibaseTask) {
      group = 'Liquibase'
      command = 'generateChangeLog'
    }
    project.task('changeLogSync', type: LiquibaseTask) {
      group = 'Liquibase'
      command = 'changeLogSync'
    }
    project.task('update', type: LiquibaseTask) {
      group = 'Liquibase'
      command = 'update'
    }

    // Create the NamedDomainObjectContainers
    def databases = project.container(Database)
    def changelogs = project.container(ChangeLog)

    // Create and install the extension object
    project.configure(project) {
      extensions.create("liquibase",
                        LiquibaseExtension,
                        databases,
                        changelogs)
    }
  }
}
```

With all of that in hand, let's take a look at the parts of the extension class itself, starting with the easiest part: the defaultDatabase property. This is an instance of the Data base class that can simply be assigned as a normal property inside the liquibase extension block. In the DSL example we sketched out, you can see this in the default Database = databases.sandbox line. This indicates to the LiquibaseTasks that they should use the Database instance called sandbox if no other database configuration is provided.

The extension class has two methods: databases and changelogs, which accept a single parameter of type Closure. Passing this closure to the configure() method of the domain object collection class will do two things: first, it will create a new instance of the domain object managed by the collection (either `Database` or `ChangeLog`). Second, it will set fields on that domain object using the property names referenced in the configuration block in the build file itself. Let's refer again to just this piece of the proposed build DSL as shown in Example 2-9.

Example 2-9. The creation and configuration of a Database domain object

```
liquibase {
  databases {
    sandbox {
      url = 'jdbc:h2:db/liquibase_workshop;FILE_LOCK=NO'
      username = 'sa'
      password = 'secret'
    }
  }
}
```

The inner `sandbox` block causes the new `Database` domain name object to be named "sandbox." (Remember, this is a *named* domain object container, so all of the objects we create in it must have names.) The property assignments inside the curly braces of the `sandbox` block are converted into property assignments on the new instance of our `Database` class.

The outer set of curly braces wrapping the `sandbox` block form the Groovy closure that is passed to the `databases()` method of the extension class. If you wanted to define additional databases for the build to access—perhaps a staging server or a production instance—those would be placed as peers to the `sandbox` definition.

The complete source code of the sketched-out plug-in is available in a GitHub Gist (*https://gist.github.com/3132622*). Remember, all of this code was typed directly into a plain Gradle build file, with no compilation or build steps required. This is a very efficient way to create a prototype, but of course a properly managed plug-in will need a build of its own, so it can be decorated with all of the appropriate testing, versioning, and release processes that attend mature software development. We'll look at this next.

Packaging a Plug-In

Converting our quick-and-dirty plug-in implementation to an independent project with a build all its own is not difficult. The process consists mainly of breaking up the classes developed in the previous section into files of their own, adding a little bit of metadata to the JAR file, and fixing up our classpath with the Gradle API. We'll look at these things one at a time.

The plug-in we built has seven separate classes packaged in the `com.august` `techgroup.gradle.liquibase` and `com.augusttechgroup.gradle.liquibase.tasks` packages. Since these are Groovy classes, we'll place them under the `src/main/groo vy` directory of the build. You can browse the source of this chapter's version of the plug-in on GitHub (*http://bit.ly/13yWKRn*).

After locating the classes there, we'll need to provide one additional file in the build to give the plug-in its ID in builds in which it is applied. In the previously sketched-out plug-in, we applied the plug-in directly by its classname with the line `apply plugin: LiquibasePlugin` at the top of the build.[5] A properly packaged Liquibase plug-in should be applied just like the core plug-ins are, with the line `apply plugin: 'liquibase'`. This plug-in ID is provided through a metadata file.

We will add a file called `liquibase.properties` in the `src/resources/META-INF/ gradle-plugins` directory of the project. This directory will automatically be included in the jar file under its `META-INF` directory. The purpose of the file is to translate from the string ID of the plug-in to the fully qualified name of the class that implements the plug-in. The file's brief contents are shown in Example 2-10.

Example 2-10. The contents of the liquibase.properties meta file

```
implementation-class=com.augusttechgroup.gradle.liquibase.LiquibasePlugin
```

Finally, the plug-in code must have a build. Naturally, we will use Gradle for this task. The full build (*http://bit.ly/14Gi1Fs*) shown in the example project contains many extra features for packaging and deployment to the Central Repository, but it can be much simpler. The main problem is solving the compile-time classpath dependency on the Gradle APIs themselves. (The plug-in also depends on Liquibase modules, but we already know how to bring in regular Maven-style dependencies from reading *Buiding and Testing With Gradle*.)

The answer to the Gradle API question is the `gradleApi()` convenience method. Declared as a compile-time dependency, it brings in all of the internal Gradle classes needed to build a project that extends Gradle itself. The completed minimum subset build is shown in Example 2-11.

Example 2-11. A simplified plug-in build file

```
apply plugin: 'groovy'

repositories {
  mavenCentral()
}

dependencies {
  groovy 'org.codehaus.groovy:groovy:1.8.6'
  compile gradleApi()
```

---

5. This line can be seen in the completed code (*https://gist.github.com/3132622*).

```
    compile 'org.liquibase:liquibase-core:2.0.3'
}
```

Conclusion

The Liquibase plug-in is a good example of a real-world product that introduces an external API to power new execution-time features and extends the build domain model in ways unique to its own domain. Hundreds of lines of build code are completely hidden inside the plug-in, and advanced functionality is introduced to the build tool as a native part of its vocabulary. And that vocabulary itself is expanded to encompass a new domain that isn't a part of the core build tool itself.

When built and packaged as a project of its own, the plug-in takes on life as a software project. We can introduce automated tests, or ideally even bake them in while we code as an integrated part of the development process. We can deploy a continuous integration server. We can apply appropriate versioning, source repository tagging, and other release management protocols. In short, this extension to the build tool brings new functionality to bear on the system, is expressed in new build language, and is engineered within the context of contemporary software development practice. This is the essence of the Gradle plug-in story, which is a very powerful story indeed.

## CHAPTER 3

Build Hooks

By itself, Gradle is a deeply customizable toolkit for creating custom build software. It comes with out-of-the-box conventions that are useful for highly standardized builds, and it exposes a rich set of APIs for introducing novel functionality into a non-commodity build as we saw in Chapter 2. But your ability to customize a Gradle build doesn't end with plug-ins.

Gradle offers you the ability to modify the execution of that program by hooking a variety of events that occur during the configuration and execution of your build. These hooks are simply blocks of Groovy code that run when tasks are added, when projects are created, and at other times during Gradle's internal configuration sequence. Also, following the patterns implicit in Groovy's own metaprogramming APIs, Gradle gives you the ability to create tasks dynamically based on its powerful *rules* feature. This chapter presents hooks and rules as a means of managing build complexity and decorating the functionality of builds whose source we do not always directly control.

The Gradle Lifecycle: A Review

Many readers of this book will be familiar with the Gradle build lifecycle, but a thorough understanding of build hooks requires that we revisit it briefly. Every Gradle build proceeds through three lifecycle phases in precisely the same order. These phases are initialization, configuration, and execution.

During the initialization phase, Gradle starts up and locates the build files it must process. Crucial during this phase is the determination of whether the build is single-project or multi-project. If it is a single project build, Gradle identifies a single build file to pass to the next phase. If it is a multi-project build, Gradle locates potentially many build files for processing in the next phase.

That next phase is configuration. During configuration, Gradle executes each build file as a Groovy script. The effect of configuration is not the actual execution of build actions—that comes next—but rather the creation of a directed acyclic graph (DAG) of task objects.[1] It is during the construction of this graph that many of the hook methods run.

The final phase is execution. During this phase, Gradle identifies the tasks in the task DAG that must be executed, and executes them in dependency order.[2] All build activities (e.g., compiling code, copying files, uploading artifacts, etc.) occur during execution. Some build hooks are evaluated during execution.

Advising the Build Graph

In the early 2000s, the paradigm of aspect-oriented programming (AOP) became a marginally popular way to manage the complexity of enterprise Java software. AOP acknowledged that programs often contained individual units of functionality—in the case of an object-oriented language like Java, these are methods—which need to be enhanced with code whose purpose is not directly related to the unit in question. For example, a method that processes a web request might need to make security assertions before it runs, or it might have to emit logging after it runs. A method that writes to the database might have to have a database context set up first and a transaction committed after.

AOP developed its own vocabulary and a small number of Java frameworks to implement it. Gradle build hooks are similar enough to AOP that some of this vocabulary is worth retaining. The code that ran before and after the original method was called *advice*. The advice code was often described as being *orthogonal* to the original code, meaning that the purposes of the two blocks of code weren't correlated in any direct way, even though the execution sequence was. The kinds of code with which one would advise application methods were called *cross-cutting concerns*. The most common tutorial examples were logging and database transaction management.

In our discussion of Gradle build hooks, we'll retain the "advice" terminology, and generally focus our examples on the sorts of orthogonal, cross-cutting concerns that have populated AOP texts for the past decade.

Advising Project Evaluation

The goal of an individual Gradle build file is to set up a Project with all of the settings and tasks it needs to give Gradle useful work to do during the build. The setup takes place during the configuration phase, and the build itself takes place during the execution phase. The `project.beforeEvaluate()` and `project.afterEvaluate()` methods

---

1. If it is a multi-project build, there is also a DAG of project objects, one for each project.

2. Dependency order means that if task A depends on task B, task B will run first.

---

are hooks to execute blocks of code before and after configuration is run on a particular project.

Example 3-1 is a trivial build that hooks the afterEvaluate event. After the build has finished evaluating, the hook checks for the presence of a grammars directory. If the directory exists, the hook creates a task called testGrammars, ostensibly to perform grammar tests on the contents of the directory. Try running the build with and without a grammars directory present. Note the output of gradle tasks in each case.

Example 3-1. Hooking project after-evaluation

```
afterEvaluate {
  if (file('grammars').isDirectory()) {
    println "'grammars' directory found"

    task testGrammars << {
      println "Running grammar tests"
    }
  } else {
    println "'grammars' directory not found"
  }
}

task helloWorld {
  doLast {
    println "hello, world"
  }
}
```

The beforeEvaluate() hook is not particularly useful in this case, since there is no way in a single build file to advise the build to do something before it is evaluated.[3] Before-hooks are only useful in the case of a multiproject build. Example 3-2 has three builds, the parent project and two subprojects. The grammar check is only performed on the subprojects—now as a before-hook—by way of the allprojects method. The configuration inside the allprojects closure is applied to all projects, and therefore has a chance to affect the subprojects, since they have not yet been evaluated at the time the closure is run. If you run the example with and without the grammar directory in all three project directories, you'll find that the parent project never gains the testGram mars task, since the beforeEvaluate hook can't run on the project in which it is read.

Example 3-2. Hooking project before-evaluation

```
allprojects {
  beforeEvaluate {
    if(project.file('grammars').isDirectory()) {
      println "'grammars' found in ${project.name}"
```

---

3. By the time the hook itself is evaluated, it's too late; evaluation has already taken place.

```
      task testGrammars << {
        println "Running grammar tests in ${project.name}"
      }
    } else {
      println "'grammars' not found in ${project.name}"
    }
  }
}

task helloWorld {
  doLast {
    println "the parent says hello"
  }
}
```

Note that the check for the file has become `project.file()` instead of merely `file()` as in the previous example. This causes Gradle to look explicitly in the individual sub-project's directory for the `grammars` directory, rather than only at the root project level.

Global Project Loading and Evaluation Hooks

The preceding examples show `beforeEvaluate()` and `afterEvaluate()` being used globally, to apply to all projects at once using the `allprojects` closure. The methods can also be applied to individual project objects just as easily, if a particular subproject needs before-evaluate or after-evaluate processing applied more surgically. However, you might find that you often have a block of processing to apply in a global sense after all projects are evaluated or, if you want to get the hook in earlier in the lifecycle than that, after all projects are loaded. This is what `gradle.projectsLoaded()` and `gradle.projectsEvaluated()` are for.

The `gradle.projectsLoaded()` method takes a closure that runs after all projects are loaded. This event fires at the end of the initialization phase, before any project evaluation has begun. Of course, not much of the Gradle object model is available for examination or configuration at this point in the lifecycle, but useful work is still possible. The `gradle` object is passed to the closure as a parameter (named `g` in Example 3-3), and can be operated upon as usual. This example shows the `buildscript` block being configured with classpath dependencies to support the loading of custom plug-ins in other builds within the project. This buildscript config—often an annoying bit of noise in small builds—is now abstracted away through the work of the `projectsLoaded()` hook.

Example 3-3. Hooking the end of the initialization phase in the settings.gradle file

```
gradle.projectsLoaded { g ->
  g.rootProject.buildscript {
    repositories {
```

```
      mavenCentral()
    }
    dependencies {
      classpath 'com.augusttechgroup:gradle-liquibase-plugin:0.7'
      classpath 'com.h2database:h2:1.3.160'
    }
  }
}
```

The `projectsEvaluated()` method similarly takes a closure that runs after all projects have been *evaluated*.[4] This event fires at the end of the configuration phase, before any build execution has begun. The entire project graph is available for inspection and manipulation at this point, and the caller can be assured that no build activity has taken place at the time the hook runs.

Build Finished

You may want to know when a build is finished, and whether it ran to completion or encountered an error. Certainly your build's command-line user interface or continuous integration framework is going to give you this feedback, but we can imagine other ways we might want to capture this status and act on it.

If the build fails, it fails because some part of the build threw an exception. A build that runs to completion without throwing an exception is considered successful. This status is reflected in the `buildFinished()` closure through the `BuildResult` (*http://www.gradle.org/docs/current/javadoc/org/gradle/BuildResult.html*) instance passed to it (Example 3-4).

Example 3-4. Hooking the build finished event

```
gradle.buildFinished { buildResult ->
  println "BUILD FINISHED"
  println "build failure - " + buildResult.failure
}

task succeed {
  doLast {
    println "hello, world"
  }
}

task fail {
  doLast {
    throw new Exception("Build failed")
  }
}
```

---

4. Recall the discussion of the Gradle lifecycle.

Running gradle succeed at the command line produces the output sequence in Example 3-5.

Example 3-5. The output of the succeed task

```
$ gradle succeed

:succeed
hello, world

BUILD SUCCESSFUL

Total time: 1.374 secs
BUILD FINISHED
build failure - null
```

Note the last two lines of the output. After Gradle reports the build has finished with Total time: 1.374 secs, our buildFinished() hook runs, reporting that that build has finished, and printing the value of buildResult.failure, which is null.

Running gradle fail at the command line captures an exception (Example 3-6). Note that the BUILD FINISHED line is still emitted, even though the build failed. Our hook runs in both cases, but only has a non-null gradle.failure property when there is a failure to report. This object is an internal Gradle API type that wraps the root-cause exception. We can inspect it to determine the cause of the failure, display it in a auto-mated build console, or simply log it.

Example 3-6. The output of the succeed task

```
$ gradle fail

:fail FAILED

FAILURE: Build failed with an exception.

* Where:
Build file '/Users/tlberglund/Documents/Writing/Gradle/oreilly-gradle-book-examples/
hooks-lab/build-finished/build.gradle' line: 14

* What went wrong:
Execution failed for task ':fail'.
> java.lang.Exception: Build failed

* Try:
Run with --stacktrace option to get the stack trace. Run with --info or
--debug option to get more log output.

BUILD FAILED

Total time: 1.453 secs
BUILD FINISHED
```

```
build failure - org.gradle.api.internal.LocationAwareException: Build file '/Users/
tlberglund/Documents/Writing/Gradle/oreilly-gradle-book-examples/hooks-lab/build-
finished/build.gradle' line: 14
Execution failed for task ':fail'.
```

Rules

Typically, a task is a specific activity with a specific name. For example, the `build` task in a Java project compiles and tests all of the code. It always does that same thing, and it is always called by the same name. It is like a particular method written into a particular class: specific and identifiable.

However, what if your task is less predictable? Cases commonly arise in which you have a certain kind of build activity to carry out that follows a general template but needs to vary with circumstances. For example, you might want a family of tasks that do the same kind of deployment, but to different hosts, or the same kind of binary repository deployment, but with different archives.

The impulse is to want to pass arguments to tasks, which isn't possible. It's easy enough to parameterize imperative task activity with a `System` property, an environment variable, or even a variable in the build script itself, but those solutions also founder on complexity considerations. They introduce extra coupling of the build to states outside the build script, and their activity is not visible at the level of the task graph—the fundamental data structure that defines a Gradle build and provides opportunities for hooking and tooling integration. In Gradle, wherever possible, we want to expose discrete and specifically named tasks to the build user. An effective way to solve the problem of dynamic task behavior within this constraint is through the use of *rules*.

Any time the build user references (i.e., executes or tries to configure) a task that doesn't already exist, Gradle consults the project's task rules. Task rules are able to respond to the request for a nonexistent task in any way they wish, but it is very common for a rule to create a task on demand based on the name of the requested task. This is useful for creating tasks dynamically based on other build configuration. If you're familiar with the `methodMissing` and `propertyMissing` facilities of Groovy or Ruby's `method_miss ing`, you've already got the idea.

The Gradle Java plug-in uses rules to provide tasks for targeted building, binary repository uploading, and cleaning. To see how rules work, let's take a look at the simplest of these three rules: the clean rule.

There is a general-form `clean` task in every Java build, which simply deletes the `build` directory. However, we might want to clean only the result of one particular task that contributes to the build. In a Java project, both the `compileJava` task and the `process Resources` task create content in the `build` directory: the compile task by putting class files by default under `build/classes/main`, and the resources task by putting them by default under `build/resources/main`. We can see this after compiling this example project (*http://bit.ly/12VLviQ*). Here we see the `build` directory after running the `build` task:

```
build
├── classes
│   └── main
│       └── org
│           └── gradle
│               └── poetry
│                   └── PoetryEmitter.class
├── libs
│   └── java-build-with-resources.jar
└── resources
    └── main
        ├── chesterton.txt
        ├── henley.txt
        ├── shakespeare.txt
        └── shelley.txt
```

Java classes have been compiled, static resources have been copied, and a JAR has been created. Simply running `clean` at this point will delete the entire `build` directory, wiping out all three of those resources indiscriminately. However, running `cleanJar` will delete only the JAR file, and running `cleanResources` will surgically remove only the `build/resources` directory.

Here's a partial listing of the build directory after running `cleanResources`:

```
build
├── classes
│   └── main
│       └── org
│           └── gradle
│               └── poetry
│                   └── PoetryEmitter.class
└── libs
    └── java-build-with-resources.jar
```

This simple example may not show particularly advanced behavior—judicious use of the `rm` command would do the same thing—but it does illustrate the power of task rules. The possibilities are compelling indeed.

Creating a Rule

Let's create a rule to ping an arbitrary server and store the results of the ping. We'll log them in the `build` directory and store them in the extended properties of the task itself, so other tasks in the build can optimize their activity based on the availability of the pinged server.

Pinging a server is a one-line operation in Java (and by extension, in Groovy), but we don't want to write a specific ping task for every server we might need to contact. Moreover, it isn't long before we take a one-line operation and start adding handling for various error cases and output formats. This is a very common story for small chunks of code that start off as simple operations, but grow in complexity over time. To keep the complexity manageable, it would be good to have that code in one place, not spread across multiple tasks containing their own customized configuration, as in Example 3-7.

Example 3-7. A rule for checking the HTTP-reachability of an arbitrary server

```
ext {
  pingLogDir = "${buildDir}/reachable"
}

tasks.addRule('Rule Usage: ping<Hostname>') { String taskName ->
  if(taskName.startsWith('ping')) {
    task(taskName) {
      ext.hostname = taskName - 'ping'
      doLast {
        def url = new URL("http://${ext.hostname}")
        def logString
        try {
          def pageContent = url.text
          // Do some regex matching on pageContent
          logString = "${new Date()}\t${ext.hostname}\tUP\n"
          ext.up = true
        } catch(UnknownHostException e) {
          logString = "${new Date()}\t${ext.hostname}\tUNKNOWN HOST\n"
          ext.up = false
        } catch(ConnectException e) {
          logString = "${new Date()}\t${ext.hostname}\tDOWN\n"
          ext.up = false
        }
        file(pingLogDir).mkdirs()
        file("${pingLogDir}/ping.log") << logString
      }
    }
  }
}
```

Presumably, using HTTP for reachability would also be accompanied by some parsing of the message body that was returned. This could easily be added to the script in an imperative way through Groovy's regular expression facilities; however, this class is already getting a little bit long. We might want to look at a better solution for managing all that imperative code.

Dealing with Imperative Rule Code

Our current rule definition relies on 18 lines of `doLast` code, which is probably too much imperative code for a well-factored, maintainable build. We can't test it, and as of this writing, most tooling does not support Groovy script development inside a Gradle build as well as it supports coding in conventional Groovy classes. The solution to this problem is the `Rule` (*http://bit.ly/1detbDn*) interface.

You may recall that every Gradle build has an embedded Groovy project in it in the `buildSrc` directory. If this project exists, it is built *prior* to running the main build, and all of the classes it generates are made available to the build script classpath. It's a convenient staging ground to begin creating a `Rule` class and some tests for it.

The basic skeleton of a `Rule` class is shown in Example 3-8. The interface specifies two methods: a getter for the description, which is used by the `tasks` task to document whatever rules are present in the build, and the `apply()` method, which will eventually create our new task. This class goes in the *buildSrc/src/main/groovy/org/gradle/examples/rules* directory of our build.

Example 3-8. The minimal Rule class

```
import org.gradle.api.Rule

class HttpPingRule implements Rule {

  String getDescription() {
    'Rule Usage: ...'
  }

  void apply(String taskName) {
  }
}
```

And now our build file becomes radically simpler. All of the imperative code has been removed from the build and placed in a source file where it belongs, so our build looks like Example 3-9 now.

Example 3-9. The build file is much smaller with a class-based rule definition

```
import org.gradle.examples.rules.HttpPingRule

tasks.addRule(new HttpPingRule(project))
```

Running `gradle tasks` will now reveal the task rule definition after the statically defined tasks are listed.

Fleshing the rule definition out a bit, we might want to add code in the `apply()` method to test the name of the task being referenced. (Remember, the point of a task rule is to capture references to tasks that don't exist, and create them if their name matches some convention.) Adding a bit more functionality to `apply()`, we have what we see in Example 3-10.

Example 3-10. A Rule class that creates a task in the apply() method

```
import org.gradle.api.Rule

class HttpPingRule implements Rule {

  def project

  HttpPingRule(project) {
    this.project = project
  }

  String getDescription() {
    'Rule Usage: ping<Hostname>'
  }

  void apply(String taskName) {
    if (taskName.startsWith('ping')) {
      project.task(taskName) {
        ext.hostname = taskName - 'ping'
        doLast {
          println "PING ${ext.hostname}"
        }
      }
    }
  }
}
```

This rule definition can be further expanded with actual network reachability code in place of the `println()` call, with that functionality comfortably factored into methods as we see fit. But more importantly, since this rule is now a class, we can test it.

If we place a JUnit or TestNG test in *buildSrc/src/test/groovy/org/gradle/examples/rules/ HttpPingTests.groovy*, the default Gradle unit test support will run the test prior to running our build. Since the topic of unit testing is already covered in *Building and Testing with Gradle* —and the `buildSrc` project works exactly like a normal project in this regard—I will invite you to explore the full example code (*https://github.com/gradle ware/oreilly-gradle-book-examples/tree/master/hooks-rule-class*) at your leisure.

Generalizing Rules Beyond Tasks

The rules we've programmed so far have all been *task rules,* or rules that create new tasks on demand. As it turns out, Gradle's rule API doesn't exist specifically at the task level, but rather at the level of the *named domain object collection* (*http://bit.ly/1ayYRY3*). That is, any named collection of things in Gradle—`SourceSets`, configurations, custom domain objects—can be created by rules.

Conclusion

When you have full control over the build source and are writing your own plug-in, often the easiest way to introduce new functionality is simply to code it directly into your custom plug-in. However, at times when build source is not available to you or is not convenient to modify, build hooks and rules provide powerful mechanisms for bringing concepts from aspect-oriented programming and metaprogramming into your build development.

## CHAPTER 4

Dependency Management

Dependencies are a formidable challenge, whether they are dependencies in a Java build, in a Ruby project, or in any other kind of system. For one thing to depend on another means accepting the liability that the depended-on thing might not be available when we need it, might be expensive to obtain, or might not work in the way we expected. Programmers are painfully familiar with these costs.

Dependencies can seem like an annoyance—indeed, much of the undeserved criticism commonly directed against Maven focuses on dependency management—but they are an unavoidable fact of a complex ecosystem and are a sign that the actors in that ecosystem are trying to divide up their labor in worthwhile ways. Therefore, Gradle embraces dependency management.

We will consider the problem of dependency management primarily from a Java perspective, since the Java community has excelled both in creating an enormous dependency management problem, and in solving it effectively. Java's early embrace of open source caused thousands of software modules to proliferate, and typical projects soon came to depend on dozens of these individual modules. The modules, in turn, depend heavily on one another.

Of course, Java dependency management solutions also apply to related languages of the JVM. Groovy and Scala builds will apply the exact same techniques shown in this chapter.

What Is Dependency Management?

You may have worked with a build that constructed the compile classpath for your compile step by blindly grabbing all the JAR files in a certain directory (usually called "lib"). Inevitably, this becomes a problem over time as the software grows. It becomes more and more costly to change or remove dependencies as it becomes increasingly difficult to determine the impact of doing so. By managing (i.e., declaring) your dependencies as part of the definition of how your software builds, the dependencies can be understood and analyzed. Having your JAR files in the *lib* directory is not the problem. It's that they are being used indiscriminately and that the relationships between them are completely opaque. Dependency management solves this problem.

It is common to see "dependency management" inaccurately equated with the automated fetching of dependencies from a remote source or even the automated fetching of transitive dependencies (i.e., dependencies of dependencies). This is a benefit of dependency management, not its essence. By declaring and modelling dependencies, tooling such as Gradle can automate working with dependencies by leveraging this information. This includes automatically fetching dependencies, detecting transitive dependency conflicts, and so on.

Gradle embraces dependency management at its core and provides excellent support for dependency automation.

Dependency Concepts

In a Gradle build script, you declare dependencies via a DSL (Example 4-1).

Example 4-1. An example of declaring a dependency

```
repositories {
  mavenCentral()
}
configurations {
  compile
}
dependencies {
  compile 'org.springframework:spring-core:3.0.5'
}
```

The preceding example shows three key concepts to Gradle dependency management: *configurations* (`compile`), *dependencies* (`org.springframework:spring-core:3.0.5`), and *repositories* (`mavenCentral()`). A "configuration" is a named grouping of dependencies. A Gradle build can have zero or more of them. A "repository" is a source of dependencies. Dependencies are often declared via identifying attributes, and given these attributes, Gradle knows how to find a dependency in a repository.

In a typical Gradle build, configuration declaration is done implicitly, and configurations fade in to a background role whose details are managed by plug-ins. However, you will not fully understand Gradle dependency management without understanding configurations thoroughly, so we'll begin with them.

Configurations

Configurations are fundamentally named buckets of files that are filled up with dependencies. A Configuration (*http://bit.ly/135LKIa*) is a special type of FileCollection. Recall that a FileCollection is a lazy specification of files that when queried (i.e., when the actual files are asked for), turns that specification into a concrete list of files. Configurations are used in a similar way, except that rather than being a specification of plain files on the filesystem, they are a specification of "dependencies" that may exist locally, on the network, or in some other abstract location. Different kinds of dependencies are *resolved* into files in different ways. While this is the fundamental role of configurations, they also provide methods for querying the declared dependencies and customizing the resolution process.

The Java plug-in introduces six configurations:

- archives
- default
- compile
- runtime
- testCompile
- testRuntime

 The archives and default configurations are actually created by the base plug-in, that is itself implicitly applied by the java plug-in. We can ignore this detail for the rest of this discussion.

The compile configuration contains all dependencies required to compile the code. When the Java plug-in's compileJava task invokes the javac compiler, it must provide a classpath. In a completely imperative build in which it's your job to build up all those command-line parameters by hand (such as might be the case in a typical Ant build), you'd have to collect all of the JAR files the compiler might need to resolve import statements in the compiled code. Assigning compile-time dependencies to the compile configuration accomplishes this same goal, since the compile classpath used by compileJava task is formed internally from the compile configuration (Example 4-2).

Example 4-2. Declaring the default configurations

```
configurations {
  compile
  runtime
  testCompile.extendsFrom('compile')
```

```
  testRuntime.extendsFrom('runtime', 'testCompile')
  default.extendsFrom('runtime')
}
```

Automated tests have different dependency requirements than the main set of source files. They will typically need every single external dependency required to compile the main sources, and will need several other modules in addition: a unit testing framework, a mocking framework, a test-friendly database driver, or others in this vein. Not only that, but automated tests also depend on the compiled output of the main source set. The Java plug-ins introduces the `testCompile` configuration to handle this collection of files. When the `compileTestJava` task runs the `javac` compiler, it looks to this configuration to set the compiler's classpath.

Often, projects will depend on modules that must be available at runtime, but need not be fetched or made available on the compile-time classpath. A common example is a JDBC driver, in which the application code is compiled against interfaces in the Java standard libraries, while the implementation is provided by a vendor. The java plug-in provides the `runtime` and `testRuntime` configurations for this purpose. These are used to create deployment archives and execute test code, but do not add to the compile-time classpath at all. The `runtime` configuration *does* contain the output of the `compileJava` task, of course, since a project's *.class* files are necessarily required to run the project.

The `default` configuration is almost never directly used in a build, but participates in project-level dependency declaration. When one build depends on another build as a subproject, Gradle's default behavior is to include all of the files in this configuration. It extends `runtime` by default.

 The Gradle war plug-in adds `providedCompile` and `providedRuntime` configurations that can be used to achieve the same effect as the Apache Maven dependency scope of `provided`. See the Gradle user guide for more information (*http://bit.ly/1drgrsV*).

Extending configurations

When we say that `default` extends `runtime` as shown in Example 4-2, we might intuitively understand the mechanism, but it's still worth some explanation. To see the details, let's look back at another case: how the `testCompile` configuration provides dependencies to the `compileTestJava` task. When compiling unit tests, we are likely to need access to every single compile-time dependency that the main source code needs, plus several other things (e.g., non-production mocks or stubs, a testing framework, etc.). Strictly speaking, `testCompile` is a superset of `compile`. Gradle supports this relationship by allowing one configuration to *extend* another.

You can see the configuration extension syntax in Example 4-2. Calling the `exten
dsFrom()` method on a configuration indicates that it will contain all of the files of the
extended configuration automatically, plus any other files you add to the extending
configuration explicitly.

The "extends" relationship between configurations is entirely mutable. If for some reason you do not want the `runtime` configuration to extend from the `compile` configuration you can simply remove it from the `extendsFrom` collection (Example 4-3).

Example 4-3. Changing which configurations a configuration extends from

```
configurations {
  runtime.extendsFrom.remove(compile)
}
```

Module Dependencies

Now that we have a scheme for organizing dependencies, let's turn our attention to the
most common kind of dependency in a Gradle build: the module. Module dependencies
are JAR files built by some other build external to the project in question. Various open-
source Java projects are good examples of modules, like Commons Logging, Hibernate,
or the Spring Framework.[1]

Modules are typically identified by a vector of three parameters: group, name, and version. The group specifies the organization responsible for the module, and is often—
but not always—a reverse domain name (like `org.apache.solr`, or `org.springframe
work`, or an outlier like `junit`). The name is a unique label for the module itself, and is
often the same as the project name (like `solr-core`, `spring-web`, or `junit`). The version
identifies which release of the project you are depending on (like `1.4.1`, `3.0.2`, or
`4.8`). These three vector elements can be expressed together in a string delimited by
colons, as shown in Example 4-4.

Example 4-4. Declaring dependencies with group-name-version strings

```
dependencies {
  compile 'org.apache.solr:solr-core:1.4.1'
  compile 'org.springframework:spring-core:3.0.5'
  testCompile 'junit:junit:4.8'
}
```

Alternatively, the three elements can be expressed as a Groovy map, with their names
explicitly called out. Example 4-5 illustrates this format. Note that only the `name` field is
required for a dependency declaration; `group` and `version` are optional.

---

1. Hibernate and the Spring Framework are actually composed of several distinct modules each. Some of those
   modules depend on one another, and some stand alone, depending only on modules outside of their respective
   frameworks.

Example 4-5. Declaring dependencies with Groovy map syntax

```
dependencies {
  compile group: 'org.apache.solr', name: 'solr-core' version: '1.4.1'
  compile group: 'org.springframework', name: 'spring-core', version: '3.0.5'
  testCompile group: 'junit', name: 'junit', version: '4.8'
}
```

By default, Gradle dependencies are *transitive*. Transitive dependencies are described more in "Maven Repositories" on page 56, but for now, all you need to know is that one module may depend on other modules, and Gradle can discover those dependencies-of-dependencies when it resolves the declared dependency against a repository. This is almost always an enormous time-saver, but sometimes it can create problems. If you depend on version 1 of module A and version 2 of module B, and module A transitively depends on version 3 of module B, you may not want Gradle to resolve that final dependency. The wrong version of a JAR file might make it into your compile or runtime classpath—and most Java developers know what a frustrating experience that can be.

Happily, you can alter transitive dependency resolution in three separate ways: you can disable it altogether (Example 4-6), you can disable individual transitive dependencies from being resolved (Example 4-7), and you can force a particular dependency to be the victor when two versions are in conflict (Example 4-8). Let's take a look at the syntax for each of these.

Example 4-6. Fetching Spring Core 3.0.6 without any of its dependencies

```
dependencies {
  compile('org.springframework:spring-core:3.0.6') {
    transitive = false
  }
}
```

Example 4-7. Forcing Spring Core 3.0.6 to dominate any other versions of Spring Core in the dependency graph

```
dependencies {
  compile('org.springframework:spring-core:3.0.6.RELEASE') {
    force = true
  }
}
```

Example 4-8. Avoiding commons-logging as a transitive dependency of Spring Core

```
dependencies {
  compile('org.springframework:spring-core:3.0.6.RELEASE') {
    exclude name: 'commons-logging'
  }
}
```

Dynamic Versions

Specifying a particular version like `3.0.6` in a dependency declaration guarantees that Gradle downloads the same module every time it runs the build, assuming that all repositories are properly maintained. This is bedrock functionality, but sometimes we'd like to make a minor adjustment to the way it works: sometimes we want Gradle to download the most recent version it can find of a given module.

Using dynamic dependencies can be risky, since a new release to a declared repository will cause a future execution of the build to produce different output artifacts—even though the build's sources didn't change at all. However, build masters may decide to use this technique for principled reasons, and Gradle supports it fully (Example 4-9). This feature interacts with the dependency cache in important ways. You should understand the cache well if you plan on using dynamic versions.

Example 4-9. Two different syntaxes for declaring dynamic dependencies

```
dependencies {
  compile 'org.springframework:spring-core:3.0.+'
  testCompile 'junit:junit:4.8+'
}
```

File Dependencies

Declaring a dependency on a Maven-style `group:name:version` vector implies that the module is probably going to be resolved against some external repository like Maven Central. However, even in a conventional project where most dependencies are managed in this way, you might still come up with a module you need to include in your build that is not available in any managed repository. It might be a vendor JAR that is only available by direct download, or a binary patch of a module that you can't conveniently deploy to any internal binary artifact repository. Regardless of the reason, Gradle is ready to help with *file dependencies*.

Since a dependency configuration is fundamentally a collection of files, it's easy enough to add more files to it by brute force. In this situation, you are likely to create a *lib* directory at the root of your project and place the files in there (Example 4-10).

Example 4-10. Declaring a dependency explicitly on a locally managed module

```
dependencies {
  compile files('lib/hacked-vendor-module.jar')
}
```

Of course, this practice may get out of hand, and you may soon find that you have a whole *lib* directory full of modules, just like the pattern typically followed by Ant builds. This isn't necessarily to be encouraged, but you can grab all of those files in one declaration, even if you've created a nested directory structure under the top-level *lib* directory (Example 4-11).

Example 4-11. Depending recursively on all of the files under lib

```
dependencies {
  compile fileTree('lib')
}
```

Project Dependencies

Separate builds in a multi-project build may depend on one another. A multi-project build is an arbitrary configuration of projects that are all evaluated together by Gradle at build time. Each build's `Project` object is related to other builds' `Project` objects in a project graph. Gradle doesn't prescribe the exact nature of these relationships, but rather provides you with a syntax to express them. When you are expressing a relationship between projects, you are really indicating that one project *depends on* another.

Looking at the multiproject example code (*http://bit.ly/14Glggc*), you recall that the project was structured as one top-level command line driver utility, plus one subproject that provided text content, and another that provided text encoding services. In this multiproject system, the top-level project depended on the two subprojects, and each of those subprojects was fully independent of each other. Note Example 4-12, and the section of the build file in the top-level project.

Example 4-12. Declaring dependencies on subprojects

```
dependencies {
  compile project(':codec')
  compile project(':content')
}
```

The code in Example 4-12 indicates that the top-level project has a compile-time dependency on both the `:codec` and the `:content` subprojects. Of course, a *project* is not a collection of files, and a dependency must eventually resolve to a file collection in order to be added to a named configuration like `compile` or `runtime`. When you depend on a project as shown in the example, Gradle assumes you mean the `default` configuration, which includes all of the compiled output of the project and all of its compile-time and runtime module dependencies. The `default` dependency configuration is covered in more detail in "Configurations" on page 49.

Of course, you might not want to grab all of the files in `default`. You might have designed a subproject's dependency configurations intentionally to publish only certain files to external projects. In Example 4-13, the `project()` method takes a map with parameters for the project `path` and the desired dependency `configuration`.

Example 4-13. Declaring an explicit configuration dependencies on a subproject

```
dependencies {
  compile project(path: ':codec', configuration: 'published')
  compile project(':content')
}
```

Internal Dependencies

The Gradle dependency DSL offers a couple of convenience methods that are particularly useful when writing code to extend Gradle itself. These are the `gradleApi()` method and the `localGroovy()` method.

If you are writing custom tasks or a custom plug-in, you will be programming Gradle's APIs directly, and will therefore have a compile-time dependency on them. This sort of dependency is similar in principle to the compile-time dependency you might have on any API you are programming, like what you might see if you are writing MapReduce jobs for execution on a Hadoop cluster or writing enterprise integration code with Apache Camel.

However, since the classes you are importing happen to be available in the same Gradle runtime package that's interpreting and executing the build, Gradle provides a method you can use to access those classes directly without having a true external dependency (Example 4-14).

Example 4-14. Depending on the Gradle API

```
dependencies {
  compile gradleApi()
  // other dependencies...
}
```

Also, while you can extend Gradle in any one of a variety of JVM languages, many Gradle developers have historically preferred do so in Groovy. Plug-ins and custom tasks written in Groovy share a common syntax with Gradle build files, and as a high-productivity dynamic language, Groovy serves the build developer well.

Gradle's Groovy plug-in makes building code in Gradle easy, but it does require one extra step: configuring a dependency on a particular version of Groovy (Example 4-15). This is normally done by assigning the dependency vector of a particular version of Groovy to a special dependency configuration called `groovy`.

Example 4-15. The configuration of a typical Groovy build

```
apply plugin: 'groovy'

// Repository declaration

dependencies {
  groovy 'org.codehaus.groovy:groovy:2.0.5'
```

```
  // other dependencies...
}
```

If you're developing code to extend Gradle itself, you don't have to declare a particular version of Groovy to use. Since Gradle's build files are Groovy scripts, every Gradle installation already contains a version of Groovy. Your custom task, plug-in, or other Gradle extension will necessarily run using the same version of Groovy as the version of Gradle for which you are writing the extension. Gradle therefore provides the `local Groovy()` method to make that local Groovy version available to your build without creating a true external dependency (Example 4-16).

Example 4-16. Depending on Gradle's internal version of Groovy

```
apply plugin: 'groovy'

dependencies {
  groovy localGroovy()
  // other dependencies...
}
```

Repositories: Dependency Resolution

Dependencies are, by definition, things external to the build. Once they are declared, this means Gradle must go get them from somewhere. In Gradle, the place dependencies are fetched from is called a *repository*.

Every Gradle project has an internal list of repositories. By default, this list is empty, but we can add to it by using the `repositories` block. Gradle uses the repositories at build execution time to fetch the build's dependencies and store them in a cache. There are three kinds of repositories currently supported by Gradle: Maven repositories, Ivy repositories, and static directories. We'll describe each one in turn, paying particular attention to its configuration DSL.

Maven Repositories

One of Maven's most valuable innovations was the Maven Central repository. Not only does it serve as a publicly accessible repository of thousands of open-source Java modules, but its structure and access protocol are open as well. Many other Maven-style repos exist on the Internet and inside corporate networks all over the world. Gradle supports these as first-class citizens.

As described in the section on module dependencies, artifacts in a Maven repository are usually identified by three coordinates: group, name, and version. This self-describing coordinate tuple was originally introduced to the Java ecosystem by the Maven repository format. In addition, modules may be qualified by their *classifier* and *type*. The classifier usually differentiates between the code, JavaDocs, and source archives. The type indicates whether the module is packaged as a JAR or some other archive format. `classifier` and `type` are often omitted from declarations, but are a supported part of the Maven repository format.

The primary value of Maven repositories is not that they offer a standard means of storing and retrieving executable code, source, and documentation over the Internet, but that they describe the dependencies between those modules as well. Each Maven coordinate, whether it corresponds to any code, source, or JavaDocs at all, always describes an XML descriptor file called a POM (Project Object Model). The POM file contains various metadata about the module, not least is the list of other modules required for the POM's module to function. By default, Gradle recursively fetches these dependencies from the repository and caches them on disk.

Since a Maven repository is nothing more than a website containing downloadable POM files and modules in a predictable directory structure, declaring a Maven repository in Gradle begins with telling Gradle the URL of the repo. The most common Maven repository is the Central repository at `http://repo1.maven.org/maven2/`; however, Gradle provides a convenience method to avoid scripting that URL directly into your build (Example 4-17).

Example 4-17. Declaring the Central repository

```
repositories {
  mavenCentral()
}
```

Central may be the most-frequently used Maven repository, but it is hardly the only one. Many other open-source Maven repositories exist on the Internet, and still more exist within the private networks of companies using Gradle for their enterprise builds. Sonatype's Nexus (*http://www.sonatype.org/nexus/*) and JFrog's Artifactory (*http://www.jfrog.com/home/v_artifactory_opensource_overview*) are two examples of products that can be used to deploy Maven-style binary repositories internally. Declaring such a repository in Gradle is a simple matter of providing the URL (Example 4-18).

Example 4-18. Declaring Maven repositories in general

```
repositories {
  maven {
    url = 'http://download.java.net/maven/2'
  }
  maven {
    name = 'JBoss Repo'   //optional name
    url = 'https://repository.jboss.org/nexus/content/repositories/releases'
  }
}
```

A Maven repository is merely a website that serves POMs and artifacts through a well-defined URL naming scheme. In some cases, we might want to obtain POMs from one website (say, a centralized corporate repo), but download build artifacts from a mirrored copy of the repo somewhere else in the network (Example 4-19). We might be motivated to do this to reduce bandwidth consumption or increase download speeds between the build server and the main repository. Regardless of our reason, Gradle makes this easy.

Example 4-19. Setting the artifact URL as distinct from the default POM URL

```
repositories {
  // Overriding artifacts for an internal repo
  maven {
    url = 'http://central.megacorp.com/main/repo'
    artifactUrls = [ 'http://dept.megacorp.com/local/repo' ]
  }
  // Obtain Maven Central artifacts locally
  mavenCentral artifactUrls: ['http://dept.megacorp.com/maven/central']
}
```

Maven famously caches all of its dependencies in the ~/.m2 directory, which is sometimes called the *local Maven repository*. Gradle maintains its own caching mechanism, but some builds might want to be able to dip into Maven's local cache to resolve dependencies. The most common use case for this is when a build needs to access a custom version of some other module, especially when that customization is itself under development and is not ready to publish to the outside world. Asking Gradle to attempt to resolve dependencies against the local Maven repo is simple (Example 4-20).

Example 4-20. Resolving dependencies against the ~/.m2 local Maven cache

```
repositories {
  mavenLocal()
}
```

Changing modules

Maven repositories can also host snapshots, or what Gradle calls *changing modules*. A changing module is one whose version is presently in a state of flux, and can't meaningfully be pegged to a single version number. Changing modules can represent code that is under active development during the workday, or code that is being rebuilt nightly given whatever state the code happens to be in at the end of the day.[2] They are still managed dependencies, but because they are subject to change, their caching semantics are different.

Normally Gradle caches a module once and never reloads it from its source repository again, since versioned modules are supposed to be immutable. However, changing modules explicitly disclaim immutability, so cached copies of those modules must be expired after some time. By default, changing modules are refetched after 24 hours in

---

2. In organizations with globally distributed teams, words like "workday" and "nightly" begin to lose crisp definition, but these remain the terms normally used to discuss builds of this kind.

the cache. You can override this default by configuring the global dependency resolution strategy.

Ivy

Apache Ivy (*http://ant.apache.org/ivy/*) was developed as an extension to the Ant build tool to provide Maven-style binary artifact management. It was never deployed as widely as Maven-style repos have been, but it sees some continued use at the time of this writing in connection with enterprise Ant builds.

In principle, Ivy repositories function very much like Maven repositories. Artifacts are identified by a vector composed of a group name, a module name, and a version. Repositories reside either at HTTP-addressable URLs or in the file system. Repository metadata, held in *ivy.xml* files, expresses transitive dependency relationships. And of course, declaring an Ivy repository in Gradle is trivial (Example 4-21).

Example 4-21. Declaring an Ivy repository using the default Maven layout

```
repositories {
  ivy {
    url 'http://build.megacorp.com/ivy/repo'
  }
}
```

Ivy differs from Maven in that its repositories do not always follow the same directory structure as one another. Maven repos have a fixed structure that follows the group, artifact, or version hierarchy, but Ivy repos may be organized along different lines. If we provide no artifact or Ivy mappings (as in Example 4-21), Gradle assumes that the Ivy repo uses the default Maven structure. However, we can define a custom layout easily enough.

Example 4-22 shows a repository that hosts all of its artifacts and *ivy.xml* files at a particular URL, but locates the JAR and Ivy files at different paths on the server. The portions inside square brackets (e.g., `[module]`, `[artifact]`, etc.) are substituted for the value of the dependency being resolved. The strings in Table 4-1 are supported.

Table 4-1. The mapping of Ivy repository variables to dependency parameters

Ivy repository variable	Dependency parameter
`[organisation]`	group
`[module]`	name
`[revision]`	version
`[artifact]`	name
`[ext]`	type
`[classifier]`	classifier

Example 4-22. Declaring an Ivy repository using a named custom layout

```
repositories {
  ivy {
    url 'http://build.megacorp.com/ivy/repo'
    layout 'custom', {
        artifact "artifacts/[module]/[revision]/[artifact].[ext]"
        ivy "ivy/[module]/[revision]/ivy.xml"
    }
  }
}
```

Moreover, a single Ivy repo may place its *ivy.xml* files and its binary modules at entirely separate URLs. If there is no common base URL between artifacts and Ivy files, use the syntax in Example 4-23.

Example 4-23. Declaring an Ivy repository using custom artifact and ivy.xml URLs

```
repositories {
  ivy {
      artifactPattern  "http://build.megacorp.com/ivy/repo/artifacts/[organisation]/
[module]/[revision]/[artifact]-[revision].[ext]"
     ivyPattern "http://build.megacorp.com/ivy/repo/ivy-xml/[organisation]/[module]/
[revision]/ivy.xml"
  }
}
```

Repository Credentials

Most Internet-based binary repositories exist to serve open-source artifacts, so they are open to everyone without authentication. Likewise, most corporate repositories exist inside trusted networks where company employees can access them freely. However, sometimes repositories have to be secured with basic username and password authentication. Maven and Ivy repositories both have mechanisms for doing so, and so Gradle has a common configuration DSL to provide these credentials in the build (Example 4-24).

Example 4-24. Adding credentials to a repository declaration, insecurely

```
repositories {
  maven {
    url = 'http://central.megacorp.com/main/repo'
    credentials {
      username 'repouser'
      password 'badly-protected-secret'
    }
  }
}
```

The problem with the naive implementation is that the password is in the build script in plain text, and is therefore checked into source control. This is, putting it mildly, not prudent password management. A better option is to put the password in an environment variable or an external properties file. Gradle automatically reads the *gradle.properties* file at startup, making build script variables out of each of the properties defined therein (Example 4-25). This is a convenient place to put passwords, as long as there is no other configuration in the file that needs to be checked into source control (Example 4-26).

Example 4-25. An example gradle.properties file containing a password

```
megacorpRepoPassword=well-protected-secret
```

Example 4-26. Adding credentials to a repository declaration, accessing the password through a properties file

```
repositories {
  maven {
    url = 'http://central.megacorp.com/main/repo'
    credentials {
      username 'repouser'
      password megacorpRepoPassword
    }
  }
}
```

Using *gradle.properties* is viable only if it can be kept out of source control though a mechanism like the *.gitignore* file or the svn:ignore property, or a similar technique appropriate for the version control system in use. If you can't afford to ignore this file due to other content you have decided to place in it, you can create a custom properties file and read it explicitly in your build script using the java.util.Properties API (*http://docs.oracle.com/javase/6/docs/api/java/util/Properties.html*) and Gradle's native Groovy scripting.

Static Dependencies

Most contemporary open-source and enterprise builds use transitive dependency management through Maven-style repos, but not every build in the world does. An older, Ant-based system might use static dependency management, where a single *lib* directory holds all of the JAR files the build needs. This might not be the preferred practice for new designs, but a prudent build migration process might only choose to attack one problem at a time, preferring to migrate core build functionality to Gradle before re-designing dependency management as well.

Other builds might use managed dependencies as much as possible, but occasionally fall back to static management for pragmatic reasons. For example, if you need to hack an old, unsupported vendor JAR at the bytecode level, or otherwise have a highly custom build of some external module, it might make more sense to control that JAR with your source code rather than publish it to a binary repository. This scenario is most likely when you don't have your own internal binary repository and module publishing mechanism established.

Whether you are managing static dependencies due to old technology or pragmatic necessity, Gradle is ready to support you. It is able to resolve dependencies against a local directory, just as if that directory were a source of Maven- or Ivy-style artifacts. Example 4-27 shows how to declare a flat directory repository.

Example 4-27. Declaring a flat directory repository

```
repositories {
  flatDir dirs: "${projectDir}/lib"
}
```

That declaration will cause Gradle to look in a directory called lib located at the project root, using the idiom common to the Ant builds of a decade ago. However, this simple declaration raises the question of how Gradle will construct filenames, since the group, name, and version metadata is now missing from the ad-hoc "repository." The answer is that Gradle builds filenames using the [group]-[name]-[version]-[classifier]. [type] formula. Some examples of how dependency declarations would be converted into strings are in Table 4-2.

Table 4-2. Examples of dependency declaration to flatDir filename mappings

Dependency declaration	Filename
'org.apache.solr:solr-core:1.4.1'	org.apache.solr-solr-core-1.4.1.jar
name: 'commons-codec', version: '1.6'	commons-codec-1.6.jar
name: 'ratpack-core', version: '0.8', classifier: 'source', type: 'zip'	ratpack-core-0.8-source.zip
name: 'commons-logging'	commons-logging.jar

As you can see, the more compact 'group:name:version' declaration, which is common when resolving dependencies against Maven repositories, might not serve as well in the flatDir case. If you have versions in your JAR filenames, you will most often use the combination of name and version in your dependency declarations. If you don't have versions in your JAR filenames, declare your dependencies with only a name attribute, and they'll resolve properly against the flat dir.

In rare cases, you might have multiple directories of static files you'll want Gradle to check when it's resolving dependencies. The syntax for declaring multiple directories is shown in Example 4-28. Note that this example also shows how to apply a name to a flatDir repo, just like we have with Maven and Ivy declarations.

Example 4-28. Declaring a flat directory repository

```
repositories {
  flatDir name: 'staticFileRepo'
          dirs: [ "${projectDir}/api-libs",
                  "${projectDir}/framework-libs" ]
}
```

Buildscript Dependencies

Most dependency and repository declarations in a build are concerned with the dependencies of the code being built: what modules are required to compile the code, to compile the tests, to run the code, and so forth. However, since a Gradle build is a Groovy program, we might choose to introduce external dependencies into the build script itself.

Let's consider an example. Suppose we have a build that has a collection of Markdown (*http://daringfireball.net/projects/markdown/syntax*) files in it, and one of the build's tasks is to convert them into HTML. This is a perfect job for a Copy task with a filter attached to it, but that filter has a lot of work to do! It has to be a full-featured Markdown parser and HTML renderer. We definitely don't want to write that code ourselves.

Happily, the MarkdownJ (*http://markdownj.org/*) project will do it for us, but now we need MarkdownJ classes to be available to us not during our project's compilation or execution, but during the execution of the build script itself. The resulting build looks like Example 4-29.

Example 4-29. Using buildscript to add to the build classpath

```
buildscript {
  repositories {
    mavenCentral()
  }

  dependencies {
    classpath 'org.markdownj:markdownj:0.3.0-1.0.2b4'
  }
}

import com.petebevin.markdown.MarkdownProcessor

class MarkdownFilter extends FilterReader {
  MarkdownFilter(Reader input) {
    super(new StringReader(new MarkdownProcessor().markdown(input.text)))
  }
}

task markdown(type: Copy) {
  from 'src/markdown'
  include '*.md'
```

```
    into 'build/labs'
    rename { it - '.md' + '.html' }
    filter MarkdownFilter
}
```

Note that the `repositories` and `dependencies` declarations inside the `buildscript` block are identical to their conventional uses as described earlier in this chapter. The one difference is the new dependency configuration: `classpath`. This is the only configuration you'll use inside the `buildscript` block. It indicates that the dependencies you're providing will be available to the classloader during the rest of the build script execution, which is exactly what we need. The line following the `buildscript` block is an import of the `MarkdownProcessor` class, which is later used to configure the copy task's filter. We could bring any resolvable modules we'd like into the build in this same way.

We can apply this same technique to load external plug-ins. As described in Chapter 2, plug-ins are merely JARs containing code that programs the Gradle plug-in API. To apply a plug-in to a Gradle build, the plug-in has to be available in the classpath of the build itself. If a plug-in is properly packaged and deployed to a binary repository like Central, we can use the `buildscript` block to make it visible to the build script (Example 4-30).

Example 4-30. Applying an external plug-in from a binary repository

```
buildscript {
  repositories {
    mavenCentral()
  }

  dependencies {
    classpath 'com.augusttechgroup:gradle-liquibase-plugin:0.7'
  }
}

apply plugin: 'liquibase'
```

Dependency Caching

It is one thing to be able to declare dependencies with a concise syntax and resolve them against a variety of artifact repositories. It is another thing entirely to do this while retaining the ability to execute builds quickly or run them when disconnected from the network. To support these goals, Gradle offers a sophisticated dependency cache, containing features no dependency management system before it has offered.

Binary repository formats like Ivy and Maven expose both metadata (e.g., *pom.xml* and *ivy.xml* files) and binary artifacts themselves (e.g., JAR files, source archives, JavaDoc archives, etc.). In an important innovation, Gradle caches the metadata and artifacts separately. This allows the dependency cache to avoid a significant category of build problems that can lead to non-repeatable builds in enterprise environments and elsewhere.

The trivial implementation of dependency caching would group all downloaded content by its identifier, which is ostensibly the standard `group:artifact:version` vector used to declare the dependency. However, the naive approach ignores the case in which different binary modules are uploaded to separate repositories with the same version number. This is always a pathological condition—the release management process should have bumped up the version number in one of those two builds—but it is nevertheless a reality in practical build environments.

Gradle caches dependency metadata (*pom.xml* and *ivy.xml*) by the group ID, artifact ID, version number, *and the repository* from which the dependency was resolved. Thus for a dependency to be "resolved" means that it has been resolved against a particular repository.[3] To fetch the metadata for `commons-codec:commons-codec:1.6` from your internal Artifactory repository and from Central are not the same operation as far as Gradle's cache is concerned. This will lead to an increase in network requests during a build, but only for small metadata files; it will only lead to more artifact downloading when such downloading is the right thing to do.

There is, in effect, one metadata cache per repository, but Gradle maintains just one artifact cache for all dependencies. Binary artifacts are stored by the SHA-1 hash code of their contents, not the repo they came from or their `group:artifact:version` metadata. Thus, all of the metadata caches share common access to a local, disk-based store of downloaded binary artifacts. In the previous example, an internal Artifactory repo may have a copy of `commons-codec:commons-codec:1.6`, and Maven Central may have the same. If they are both legitimately serving the same JAR—as defined by both files sharing the same SHA-1 hash code—then Gradle will only download the binary artifact once, and store it in one place on disk. Gradle relies heavily on hashes to optimize download performance; when resolving a dependency, it will first attempt to download the much-smaller SHA from the repo, skipping the download if it determines that it already has that content in the artifact cache.

There are a couple of important command line switches that impact the way Gradle uses its dependency cache. The `--offline` switch tells Gradle to use cached dependencies, and not to attempt to re-resolve anything (e.g., changing dependencies) against networked repositories. This is useful when working without a network connection or when a needed repository is offline. The `--refresh-dependencies` switch, by contrast, forces Gradle to go to the network to re-evaluate and re-fetch all dependency metadata. It will not download redundant modules if an artifact with the matching SHA-1 is

---

3. A repository is defined as a URL, a type (e.g., Maven, Ivy, etc.), and a layout. All Maven repos have the same layout, but Ivy repos may differ.

already present in the artifact cache. This can be useful to ensure that you are building against the very latest of any changing or dynamic dependencies.

Configuring Resolution Strategy

Every dependency configuration has a resolution strategy associated with it. In most builds, this strategy operates behind the scenes and out of the view of build masters and developers alike, but dependency problems can arise that require its customization. At present, there are three parts of the strategy that you can change: what to do when a version conflict arises, whether to force versions of certain artifacts, and what caching semantics to apply to changing and dynamic dependencies. Let's look at these in turn.

Failing on Version Conflict

Since Gradle resolves dependencies transitively, two independently declared dependencies may result in conflicting versions of some module they both depend on. For example, a web form processing API may depend on `commons-collections:commons-collections:3.2.1`, whereas an older vendor-specific enterprise integration module may rely on `commons-collections:commons-collections:2.1`. Gradle will detect that different versions of the same module are in the dependency graph, and by default it will choose the newer version. However, building the enterprise integration module with Commons Collections 3.2.1 might not work. You might want to know about the conflict and fail the build. You can do this, either globally or on a per-configuration basis, as in Example 4-31.

Example 4-31. Failing the build when a dependency version conflict is detected

```
configurations.all {
  resolutionStrategy {
    failOnVersionConflict()
  }
}
```

Forcing Versions

Following the prior example, you may determine that the modules that declare the newer dependency are simply trying to stay up-to-date in their dependency metadata, but are in fact backward compatible with the older version of Commons Collections. Rather than defaulting to the new version or failing the build, you might want to force Gradle to use version 2.1 instead of 3.2.1 (Example 4-32).

Example 4-32. Forcing a particular version of a given dependency

```
configurations.all {
  resolutionStrategy {
    force 'commons-collections:commons-collections:2.1'
  }
}
```

Cache Expiration

Statically declared releases like `commons-collections:commons-collections:3.2.1` and `commons-collections:commons-collections:2.1` are immutable artifacts. They are published to repositories on the network, and can be downloaded from those repositories through the mechanisms we've covered so far. Once downloaded, they are highly amenable to caching, since they can be identified uniquely and they never change. However, dynamic dependencies and changing dependencies are not immutable, and so their caching semantics are subject to more customization.

Dynamic and changing modules are still cached, but since the artifact can become out-of-date with respect to their identifiers, Gradle invalidates the cached versions after some period of time. By default, both types of cached artifacts expire after 24 hours, but both timeouts can be set to arbitrary periods (including zero) using the `resolution Strategy` block. Again, you can change these settings on a per-configuration basis, or uniformly to all configurations as shown in Example 4-33.

Example 4-33. Setting the dependency cache expiration policy.

```
configurations.all {
  resolutionStrategy {
    cacheDynamicVersionsFor 1, 'hour'
    cacheChangingModulesFor 0, 'seconds'
  }
}
```

Conclusion

Gradle has rich and customizable support for the current state of the art in dependency management as it has evolved in the world of the JVM. It fully supports Maven and Ivy repositories, and pragmatically adapts to legacy builds that use static dependency management. Moreover, its dependency caching feature helps solve difficult build repeatability problems that afflict real-world enterprise builds. There are few dependency management scenarios it can't handle natively or be adapted to through a few easy customizations.

Afterword

If you've read through this short book and coded along with the examples, you've got a solid grounding in many of the topics you'll need as a Gradle power user. There is always more to learn, but understanding Gradle's philosophy of file operations, its amazing plugin API, its build metaprogramming model, and its dependency management scheme will get you most of the way you need to writing the intelligent custom builds the future calls for.

To develop a custom build is to develop custom software. It is not merely to cobble scripts together as a second-class activity, subservient to the "real" software that drives the business domain. If you are using the techniques you've learned here, you are coding in the highly specialized domain of your build. That body of software you create supports every other line of code your team writes.

It is my hope that the material in this book moves you closer to mastering Gradle, using this build tool to add more and more value to your software delivery pipeline as your team's build and deployment practices continue to evolve. This process is important, and so your continued education in Gradle is important. I'm pleased to have offered another small contribution to this end.

About the Author

Tim Berglund is a full-stack generalist and passionate teacher who loves coding, presenting, and working with people. He is founder and principal software developer at the August Technology Group, a technology consulting firm focused on the JVM. He is a speaker internationally and on the No Fluff Just Stuff tour in the United States, co-presenter of the best-selling O'Reilly Git Master Class, and co-president of the Denver Open Source User Group. He has recently been exploring build automation, non-relational data stores, and abstract ideas, like how to make software architecture look more like an ant colony. He lives in Littleton, Colorado, with the wife of his youth and their three children.

Colophon

The animal on the cover of *Gradle Beyond the Basics* is a Belgian shepherd dog (Tervuren).

The cover image is from Shaw's General Zoology. The cover font is Adobe ITC Garamond. The text font is Adobe Minion Pro; the heading font is Adobe Myriad Condensed; and the code font is Dalton Maag's Ubuntu Mono.

Have it your way.

Milton Keynes UK
Ingram Content Group UK Ltd.
UKHW050109060224
437317UK00012B/608

9 781449 304676